Beginnings Without End

Other books by the same author

Voices and Visions
Telling Your Story (with Anne Valley Fox)
To a Dancing God
Apology for Wonder
Gabriel Marcel

Beginnings Without End

Sam Keen

1817

Published in San Francisco by
HARPER & ROW, PUBLISHERS
New York, Hagerstown, San Francisco, London

For Howard Thurman
teacher and friend who
has brooded over my becoming
for a score of years.

The theme photograph used is from "Trees" by Andreas Feininger. Copyright © 1968 in all countries in the International Copyright Union by Andreas Feininger. Reprinted by permission of The Viking Press, Inc.

First Harper & Row paperback edition published in 1977.

Library of Congress Catalog Card Number: 75–9321
ISBN: 06–0642652

The text of this book is printed on 100% recycled paper.

77 78 79 80 81 10 9 8 7 6 5 4 3 2 1

Contents

A year before the outward events
that changed my life I had a dream:
A man walked into my room. He was strong
and beautiful, a seasoned man who had fought
many battles in the dark jungles of the world.
He came over, sat on the edge of my bed,
and said:
"I have learned one important thing in my life—
how to begin again."
Sam Keen in Beginnings Without End

"The life span of man running toward death would inevitably
carry everything human to ruin and destruction if it were not
for the faculty of interrupting it and beginning something new,
a faculty which is inherent in action like an ever-present reminder that men, though they must die, are not born in order
to die but in order to begin . . . Action is, in fact, the one
miracle-working faculty of man, as Jesus of Nazareth . . . must
have known very well when he likened the power to forgive to
the more general power of performing miracles, putting both
on the same level and within the reach of man."
Hannah Arendt in The Human Condition

Endings: Invitation to a Journey

Nearing the mythical age of forty I fell in love with a young woman, and left a home that had been rich in care, in fighting, in love-making on Sunday mornings, in shared memories of the birth of children, in the myriad details that weave the lives of solitary individuals into a single family. Whether divorce was an act of courage or betrayal remains moot. Beyond question I found myself at mid-life in a radical crisis; like a plant whose roots had been torn from accustomed soil. One rainy morning I awoke alone in an apartment in San Francisco with the realization that my marriage had finished, my wife had remarried, my children were living far away, my lover had departed and my academic career had been abandoned. My emotional capital seemed exhausted. My past looked infinitely richer than any future I might create. Depression lurked and easily invaded any empty moment. I had either to surrender to despair or mourn the death of my old life and find some way to begin again.

For many months I was a victim of bitter confusion. And then gradually my struggle to create or discover a new life began to take form. I came to the realization that

I was living out a myth that gave my pain, conflict and dislocation a meaning. With a sense of relief I now understood the central message of the Christian myth: You must die in order to be reborn. I had been living the story of the hero who must descend through the dim winter light into the underworld of chaos and pain before he can spring up into the miraculous light of the ordinary. Through discovering that the myth which informs my life with meaning involves the belief that all life is a process of beginnings without end, I found the terrors of a mid-life identity crisis becoming transformed into an adventure.

During three years of intense inner turmoil and change I wrote, almost daily, memos to myself. Whenever I found a way to move from despair to hope, or numbness to anger, or sorrow to laughter I tried to capture the insight in an aphorism, a paragraph, a story or an essay. This book began from notes and fragments I left beside the trail to mark my journey. When I was past the crisis, I retraced my steps and filled in descriptions of the roads and twisting lanes that led me from one point to the next.

I share this log of my travels because I think it may be helpful to others who are on a similar adventure. Each person's journey involves both unique circumstances and a common map. My particular path is only a variation of a way that is universal. Any radical turning point in the life of a person or a culture—adolescence, the death of a child or friend, crippling disease, divorce, retirement, defeat in war—involves a death of the old and, hopefully, rebirth of the new. Most primitive peoples had rites of passage to help individual members of the tribe ritualize and dignify the identity crises that occur to us all approximately once each decade. Among the Plains Indians, for instance, adolescent boys went through ordeals, vigils, and fasts in quest of a vision that would give them a name and guiding image. Until such time as we can recreate communities with the wisdom to celebrate these stages of the human journey perhaps the best we can do is share our experiences of the road. This book is offered to anyone who feels the need to begin again. It is not so much the story of my journey as it is a report of places where I found an oasis, a helping spirit, a devouring demon, a rushing river or a tree with magical apples.

Winter

Descent into
Darkness

nce upon a time, before the journey began, Person (who may have been either a man or a woman) lived securely in a world of moderation and self-assurance. S/he was ordinary enough, neither a hero nor a heroine, perhaps a tired housewife or a slightly bored professor. In the Average World everything appeared to be under control. Pleasantness was the rule of the day and a smile was the passport to acceptance.

Then one day, quite suddenly, the earth trembled and Dark Forces sucked Person into the Underworld of the Unconscious. There s/he was assaulted by Irrational Powers. Terror, Pain, Loneliness, Insanity and Impotence rose up with such force that Person was tossed around like a piece of flotsam on the Chaotic Sea of Emotion.

At first Person surrendered to the storm, but then s/he grew tired of being a Victim of blind currents and impersonal powers. Anger rose like a cleansing fire. A heroic power seemed to invade Person and s/he siezed the Sword of Aggression and did battle with the alien powers who had previously ruled the ordinary world. Without a smile s/he laid waste The Authorities of the Old Order who had enforced the Taboo against Self-Knowledge. Father and Mother were killed in the rebellion. Propriety, Moderation and the Illusion of Control vanished in the middle of the battle.

And for the first time Person looked with no-longer-innocent eyes on the faces of Good and Evil. It was frightening and exciting and Person felt both like an ancient hero and a little child. S/he saw both the wonder and the horror of this New World and knew its wildness could never be domesticated by The Authorities of the Average World. Word, Explanation and Technique no longer satisfied Person nor created an illusion of understanding and security. No, for at the heart of things Person saw there was The Holy Void, a black hole in inner space where Chaos and Creativity lived.

With the old securities and comforts of home gone Person grew tired of being heroic and began to feel terribly lonely and vulnerable. Exhausted from battle, divorced from the riches of the past and the protection of the Giants of the Average Old World, Person lay down in the Tomb of Nothingness. And the Void of Winter engulfed everything.

1

The End of Time

Begin with an ending, a death, a failure. In a crisis old patterns don't work anymore. All of my past virtues have become vices. Hard work, commitment and willpower don't serve me well in this time. I must face the soft feelings of grief and confusion. I must remain vulnerable to the trembling.

Human life comes from the humus, that "brown or black complex and varying material formed by the partial decomposition of vegetable or animal matter; the organic portion of soil." To be human is to remain humble, rooted in a past that is always dying, and to flower into some unknown future. We are always ending and beginning at the same time. Grief and hope are Siamese twins.

In a time of crisis plunge into the "negative" emotions that are usually repressed or ignored. The journey of the hero begins with the descent into the realm of the demons.

FEAR AND TREMBLING

Emergency Map: In an identity crisis expect something like this: To get to the Kingdom of the Sun learn to be at home in the dark. The highway starts low. To get high, go deep. To come alive again, pass through three dark zones: chaos, death and pain (crucified, dead, buried and descended into hell). In the initial crisis (which can be triggered by anything: marriage or divorce, moving to a new city, a birth or death in the family, retirement) the personality is torn apart. Confusion reigns and fog covers the landscape: Who am I? Where am I? Where am I going? Then comes a time of numbness. The body freezes to protect us against further pain; the character armor tightens to guard us against the onslaught of the strange, new world. Our defenses keep us from feeling anything—terror or hope. To move toward Spring live through midwinter. Invite awareness. Open your eyes to your blindness. Feel deadened nerves. Look for death (gaining on you) just a step behind nervous preoccupation. Look for signs of defeat in fallen shoulders and collapsed chest. Look for despair in the short, anxious rhythm of breathing. Look for grief in the breath that catches in the hollow of the chest. Look for depression in the dullness of the eyes and the blues in the night. Look for resignation in the absence of desire—impotence and frigidity.

Once the numbness of death is acknowledged currents of new life can begin to pass through the scar tissue—sparks of new awareness, power, delight. The pain of coming alive is mixed with the pleasure. It is always a surprise when it begins to happen.

de / light
in
the
dark

Name the demons. In the old myths the hero gained power over evil spirits when he could call them by name. In any crisis an undifferentiated herd of negative emotions tramples us, down into the dark places where the corridors of fear, helplessness and despair merge.

Divide and conquer. Differentiate:

Anxiety
Fear
Terror
Hate
Anger
Longing
Grief
Loneliness
Despair
Fatigue
Impotence
Ambivalence

So long as you do not make distinctions between emotions you will remain a one-feeling person, monotonous like a one-horse town or a one-string fiddle. You will respond to all threats with a single emotion.

Love all the animals in the zoo. Paint with all the colors on the palette.

Failure gave me a chance to start over.

᪥

Death, the final failure. The end. Telos or finis? I don't know. Begin with the end. My ignorance is a small, but true, comfort. Begin with all the illusions I cherish to protect me against what I imagine are the jagged edges of reality. (Sliding down the razor blade of life.) The evasions, defenses, avoidances. Death lurks beneath the symbols ($) of my security, the grasping I call love, the bondage I call commitment, the frenzy I call creativity. Death, like an old black-clad Viet Cong warrior, hides behind the bushes of my consciousness. He tricks me into fighting the wrong enemy. One of my favorite strategies for avoiding D - - - - is to focus on the fear that my woman will abandon me. I place the mask of the unthinkable terror over the living face of the one I love. How can I accept death without dying? How can I touch without grasping, love without placing the expectations of permanency upon the loved one? If I could learn that nothing could save me I might stop looking for a savior.

᪥

Free/doom.
Free to die
Free to live.

᪥

Anxiety: A/void/dance

᪥

The fear of abandonment is the gateway to discovery of the self. At the edge of the abyss where I face my final aloneness I long for security. I look for someone to hold on to, to make everything all right. The more I grasp the more I fear losing my security blanket.

Let loose. Fall free. On the other side of the terror is the courage to live as a single one.

Embrace fear. Invite it into the house of awareness. Hold it gently until it is ready to leave. Push fears out the front door, disown them or try to conquer them by will power and they will only return by the back door, like rejected children seeking love. I am the father of my fears; they will only depart when I have learned to accept them.

Fear is a protean demon-god. It assumes a thousand disguises: the fear of failure, abandonment, ridicule, sex, high places, sharks. Unmask it and there is only a single fear.

You can't exorcise ghosts by avoiding graveyards.

There is a moment in the downward spiral of any "negative" emotion (fear, anxiety, despair) when an escape route opens up. Stop running away from the dreaded thing. Turn slowly. Face it. Walk deeper into the anxiety and know the pain. Cease resisting (evil?). Breathe deeply. Soften your body and mind and let the full force of the rejected feeling into your awareness. Listen. Be attentive to the voice of the pain. Invite it to speak to you about your life. What is it trying to tell you? "Negative" emotions are much like repressed and dispossessed peoples in the body-politic. They cease to be destructive when they are invited into full participation in the commonwealth. Repress them and there will be insurrection rather than resurrection.

When I plunged down the open maw of the monster I grabbed his tongue as I fell and turned him inside out. I found something I desired hidden under my fear.

Where I tremble I find the lost scent of the sacred. At the raw edge of fear and desire (*tremendum et fascinans*) I face the unkown mystery. Near the site of the fear and trembling is a burning bush. Or a demon? Or both. When did I tremble last? The sanctuary is always on shaky ground. God loves earthquakes.

Play it cool and you will soon be frigid. Avoid all wild places and you will never feel anything. When I look at the things that frighten you they seem insignificant to me; but when I look into my own wilderness I tremble. After the shaking comes the warmth.

Insecurity is a part of acting, because tragedy may accompany decisions. To love one person I must neglect another. To follow one path I must leave another unexplored. Each decision is a castration; the cutting off of a possibility. And the other way might have been more satisfying. A moral person is one who acts and takes responsibility. My way is littered with mistakes and unchosen options.

PAIN AND ANGER

Half of wisdom is knowing how to manage pain. Psychosomatic medicine has suggested that 90 percent of mental anguish and possibly 70 percent of physical pain is chosen. We must assume the human animal has a love affair with pain. Why do we love this enemy?

Why are known hells preferred to strange heavens?

Why do I expect pain rather than pleasure when I get close to another person or to my own depths? Why do I leave a pleasure feast when I am still hungry? My old pains are such familiar friends. And the promise of the vast unknown is always mixed with terror.

Pain is often the angry voice of the flesh crying out, demanding attention. It signals the presence of disenfranchised minority (a neglected need, feeling, memory, energy) within the politics of the body. So long as the pain is repressed, by tranquilizers or stoic willpower, the strangers within will remain angry and will destroy the tranquility of the whole.

In the healing process pain may give birth to anger, red hot anger—the impulse to strike out and destroy all that stands in the way of desire. In the quest for liberation there is a moment when the volcano erupts and molten lava flows over the surrounding countryside. It burns a path to the sea, destroying any living thing that stands in its way. At first the anger may be misdirected. The old order must be destroyed before a new one will arise. The voice of anger shouts: "No! Don't tread on me! Get off my back! Death to the oppressors!" The heart attacks and threatens to destroy everything if its demands are not met. If we ignore the voice of pain nature may use death to remind us that life must be filled with pleasure and satisfaction, or else!

I escape from pain when I discover what I like about it. What is so good about grief? What is the payoff?

These are great gurus:
      pain
          and
              pleasure
                    loneliness
                        and
                            love.

LONELINESS AND SOLITUDE

Most suffering is rooted in the fear of being alone. And what is there to fear? If I am alone I am in bad company. I attack myself with self-consciousness or burden myself with a squadron of oughts, bully myself into striving. For most of my life I have fled from solitude, seeking comfort in the arms of a woman, the company of friends or the applause of the public.

When the modern world popped out of the womb of the machine into the incubator of the city, the human person was torn out of the nurturing context of the tribe. "Individuality" is a modern dis-ease whose symptoms are loneliness, and self-consciousness. But the only way to cure the dis-ease is to go deeper into it. (Rafting down the rapids of the Colorado river; thrown overboard and sucked down into a whirlpool; instinct pushes me to struggle to get to the surface; but I go deeper and the river spits me out downstream in calmer water.)

What are the building blocks of which the prison of the ego is constructed? I, I, I. One is one and all alone and evermore shall be so. No one to trust except me. And I am untrustworthy. I am afraid to stay in here by myself and afraid to lower my drawbridge and let the world come in. I circle endlessly in solitary confinement looking within myself for the bedrock of my security and excitement. Yet the more I look the deeper I fall into obsessive self-consciousness. I bore downward into my already troubled psyche and watch myself carefully. Isolated in the circle of my own consciousness. It is painful and safe in here. No one can take the tragic glory of my self-inflicted wounds from me. I am the mock hero in this war between me, myself and I. And you are outside; a stranger; an alien, an enemy. I command the San Simeon of my imagination; a castle set on a hill. The logical end of the modern individual is: destructive self-consciousness (I am watching me) or paranoia (they are watching me).

What if: The modern romance with "the individual" is finished?

What if: Our atomic separateness, our isolated Marlboro man independence is an illusion?

What if: We are not alone in the world?

What if: Communion is a more fundamental fact of reality than isolation?

What if: The Western "self" is an abberation?

What if: Psychology, which aims at autonomy and strengthening the ego, is a manifestation of the dis-ease for which it purports to be a cure? (The doctor is reinfecting the patient.)

What if: "Sanity" and "maturity" in our society means

the ability to adjust to the crippled circuit of prison life?

What if: Neurosis and psychosis are diseases to cure diseases—antibiotics in the body-politic?

What if: The religious perspective is the only one that heals?

What if: Things are already together; the moving principle of the cosmos is the drive toward reconciliation of contradictions; or is it love, love, love, love, love, love, love, ad infinitum, that rules the whirling atoms?

I feel considerable embarrassment in asking such tender-minded questions. Even to contemplate a nonalienated form of consciousness threatens the red badge of courage I was awarded by the Existentialist Philosophers Association for manfully stomaching my nausea and accepting the truth of my ontological aloneness. The modern intellectual's masculinity has been certified by his nihilism. Our dignity comes from the wounds we have suffered in our metaphysical isolation. But what if these wounds are self-inflicted? Then the courage of individualism begins to look like masochism. Even questioning the possibility of a softer and more comforting view of the cosmos as communion seems like heresy to my modernity. If we were not alone in the depths of our consciousness, who would we be? Without our wounds would we have our dignity? And why are we so terrified of "homecoming"? Of contentment? Of the communion of all consciousness? It does appear increasingly likely that plants and dolphins and all living things are linked in a communication network. And that adds to my suspicion that love does make the world go round.

When aloneness is not tainted with the odor of abandonment, it is sweet as desert air after a storm.

Gifford gave me a Zuñi fetish for Christmas; a small totem animal carved from jade—the lone wolf. I have been encapsulated in the noise and speed of my mind, although seldom physically alone and silent. Solitude begins when I remain quiet and cease to project my fears and hopes on others. Until recently I secretly believed some outward circumstance or other person would relieve me of the anxious burden of my life. Someday the perfect woman, the perfect house in the sunshine by the sea, the perfect work would make me happy. Now I suspect that outward circumstances will never raise the water level of my happiness any higher than it has reached in the privacy of my consciousness. Dis/illusionment returns the power of happiness to me and brings the marvel and the terror of solitude.

Allow yourself to get hungry before eating.
Loneliness is hunger for another person.

I invite others into the citadel of my solitude.
But I do not give it into their keeping.

MADNESS AND ALIENATION

Madness comes from isolation, from being an alien in a hostile land. Not from solitude.

Madness or psychic play? Schizophrenia or psychic mobility? It all depends on the definition of the multiplicity that is within each of us. And definition depends on a

15

community. When my multiple selves are affirmed and enjoyed by others, I love the richness of the play. When they are not, my complexities seem to be signs of madness, evidence that I have failed to construct an identity. Then I am tempted to work desperately to make myself into a single and consistent thing.

Madness is often only anger in isolation, not the glorious dancing of Zorba or the inspired possession of the shaman. In the garden variety neurosis the world is only a stage prop in a private theater, where I replay the old melodrama: The Story of a Victim. The idea of introducing a new play fills me with horror. The new is to be avoided. The stranger is an enemy. In paranoia, I shrink inward and become fearful of all that is outside. You are not there because there is neither you nor a there. (I am the only person in the parenthesis of my self-consciousness. You and the world do not really exist except in me, me, me.)

When the circle of self and madness tightens, the prison walls close in ("The Pit and the Pendulum") and life is reduced to solitary confinement.

MADNESS	SANITY
(I)	We
Etherialization. All flesh become words, all matter is reduced to what is in my mind.	Incarnation. All words take flesh and become deeds. I have intercourse with a strange world.
Life is a command performance in a private theater before an audience of missing ghosts.	Life is a meeting with erotic persons, places and things.

You're not free when you are
always eye(I)ng your self.

I see today (after hours of fighting and more hours of
walking) how madness is a choice, a decision about a
direction, a way of not being in the world.

The meaning of madness:

I will turn inward and make the world coincide with my
fantasies, desires, feelings.

I am passive and have no control over the images,
thoughts and desires that sweep over me.

Other people have power but I do not. I can only put
myself in their control. Others can. I can't.

"I can't" is a decision, a way of exercising power by deny-
ing power, a way of sealing myself within the sovereign
kingdom of the isolated ego and handing the responsibility
for the world over to others.

Sanity requires a recurring decision to leave the fantasied
world of single and secure satisfaction and come again and
again into the world of plural satisfactions and plural pains.
There are more things in this world than philosophers or
neurotics can dream of.

Jogging on a pier in San Francisco. A fisherman starts a
long cast. As his pole comes back, the lure with three-
pronged hooks whips dangerously close to my eye. My
brain registers DANGER. I veer aside with my best broken-
field running step. My mind immediately translates the
impulse DANGER into the paranoid judgment: He intends to
do me evil. Immediately I catch my paranoia and correct
my judgment: There is danger here but he intends me no

17

evil. The transition from alienation to trust takes place in a mili-second. Paranoia must be countered with trust a hundred times a day.

Paranoia—the archetypal dis/ease. Luther called it un-faith. "They" are against me, trying to harm or kill me. The whole context of my existence is dangerous, fearful, hostile. Others are enemies, the world an extended battleground. With this stance love becomes impossible. Sex is a form of combat. Hell is other people.

"Self-consciousness is the lowest degree of paranoia" (Fritz Perls). Someone (me) is always watching me. This stance turns the whole world into a stage, and my life into an anxious performance. What if I don't perform well? Don't please the audience? And of course I can't please them because their eyes and mine are both critical and perfectionistic. In self-consciousness I am always judging myself. I am inadequate and "they" are powerful but hostile. Sooner or later I feel the hostility in the watching eyes and come to hate them—"Goddamn your eyes." If I know the watching eyes are my own I may try to put them out—like Oedipus—to destroy the enemy within who kills spontaneity and feeling. Better darkness than the sterilizing light of self-consciousness. If I project the disapproving eyes onto an "other" I can then erect defenses against all those who are in on the "plot" against me (most everyone).

The opposite of paranoia is the assumption that the "other" is a friend. I may enter the darkness and mystery of the other (man, woman, world, God) without armoring my body with tension or anesthetizing it by fear. That which is strange is approached in friendship, not aliena-tion. We are in this thing together.

Paranoia is compounded of speed, heat, noise and incessant thinking. All things must be connected and I am at the center of the matrix of meaning. And I will only be secure if I can fit all the pieces of the puzzle together. My mind works overtime searching for explanations. Why? Why? Why? It asks questions and interrogates. But it does not listen. A drop of calm, a moment of silence, a thimblefull of the Void is enough to reverse the paranoid movement of the mind. Stop. Look. And listen.

Thinking
Chattering to myself
Avoiding silence.

2

The Death of Old Gods and Goddesses

There is a time for destruction.

Self-knowledge begins with a crime.

Adam ate the apple. Prometheus defied the gods.

Kill the old gods, challenge the authorities, rupture the nurturing matrix of childhood.

Before the hero may return to the luminous world of ordinary reality he must kill giants and wrestle with demons.

Before I can achieve autonomous maturity I must destroy both the virtues and vices I inherited from my parents.

To be born again is to take the responsibility for being the father and mother of my own values.

My parents were good and strong. My father mixed stern discipline with warmth and generosity. My mother spared no effort to inform her childrens' minds with the vision of truth she saw and lived. They both had a touch of fanaticism, or at least more passion than was convenient in middle class neighborhoods. But they were not hypocrites. They lived by the values they spoke. Their nurturance was rich and their devotion to the clan fierce. I know what it means to be a member of a family. And, how difficult it is to break away from the familial bonds. Strong parents produce children who are destined either to conform to their values or to wage a fierce battle to escape the mold. I loved my parents; therefore I kill them in order to become myself.

To be reborn discover a new father and mother.

Recreate the past by alchemy.

Choose to be who you have been.

Recreate yourself as agent rather than victim.

Presto——change resentment into gratitude.

Use memory for re/creation; make a playground of the past.

Forgiveness is the key to re/creation of the past and the future. Without forgiveness there is only the endless repetition of the cycle of resentment-retaliation-reaction. Injuries must be recognized; pain fully felt; forgiveness offered before anything new can happen. So long as I blame my parents I remain a child. I cannot enjoy daily bread until I have forgiven my (imaginary) debtors. Time is either a gift (a present) or a debt to be repaid by a guilty creditor.

There is no forgiveness without acknowledging injury and pain. Only the guilty can be forgiven. The psychological fact is: every child had an unhappy (and happy) childhood; all parents injured their children. When I forgive my parents for their failures to be gods I discover our common humanity. Cease blaming them for my pains and faults and I remember a new past, a happy childhood. And I find a new future filled with personal authority. We cease being impotent children when we claim the power to be responsible for the world. We become the giants and heroes of the present age.

GUILTY/NOT GUILTY:
THE PSYCHE AS COURTROOM

In the transition from childhood to maturity we act out a drama of judgment. The transfer of authority from outside the self to inside takes place in the courtroom. Play with the analogy: the psyche as courtroom. (It is also theater, circus, city, computer, et cetera.)

The prosecutor proclaims in a loud and righteous voice: "You have broken the law. You have departed from the sacred way. You are guilty and your life is forfeit." Listen to the voice carefully and you will hear that it is a composite of the voices of all the authorities of the old order, the sacred shaman of the past: father, mother, boss, those higher on the ladder of status than yourself, the heroes of tradition. They all accuse you.

The defense attorney, oozing charm and apparent goodwill, insists on your absolute innocence: "You have done nothing wrong. Whatever fault and guilt there is falls on others. After all, you had a difficult childhood, and society is rotten, and 'they' have power and you don't. You are innocent." Behind the voice of innocence is the timid, over-whelmed child who is afraid to admit any responsibility for fear of being judged totally guilty and annihilated by the stern protectors of the law.

For a time the charge—guilty!—and the countercharge—not guilty!—are hurled back and forth, and the psyche is immobilized in the battle beween absolutes.

The jury is brought in to decide the case. It includes representatives of the whole human community past, present *and future*. The jury incorporates wider ranges of experience and values than those of the parent and child who are locked into the battle between guilty and not guilty. On my jury sit all those persons of wisdom and compassion whose insight and love I need in evaluating my life, all those whom I invite to help me distinguish between better and worse: Jesus, Socrates, Augustine, Kierkegaard, Luther, Hume, Zorba, Marcel, Fritz, Hannah, Howard, Jane, Bob, Lael, Gifford, Sigmund, Carl, and many more. From this jury I get some realistic sense of my own power and responsibility. I learn what things within myself and the world I may reasonably expect to change and what crippledness and limitation I am (prob-ably) fated to live with. I borrow their eyes and hearts to look at myself. When I know which are my flat and which my rounded sides, I can determine the extent of my guilt for acts I have committed or omitted.

The judge, the impartial fair witness, hears the case pro and con, accepts the judgment of the jury and passes sentence. His task is to determine what actions I must take in the future to minimize or compensate for what-ever injury my acts have caused. His concern is that I act in a new way, accept my power and responsibility to change things and return to the community with no crip-pling burden of unresolved guilt.

Liberals, humanists, Dionysians, and warm, flowing occultists do not like the analogy of the law court. It seems legalistic, calculating and morbid to them. Why not be spontaneous and act on feeling alone? Why not be rid of the concept of guilt? Liberal psychology believes it dignifies persons by eliminating the idea of guilt. I believe the opposite is true.

I am convinced (I may be wrong) that the drama of guilty/not guilty must be played out before the psyche is released from bondage to infantile shame and impotence. The alternative to determining my degree of guilt and responsibility is not to live in innocence but to exist in a state of unspecified shame. In shame we are dominated by the blind power of the authorities and elders. We cringe before the threat of disapproval and lack the courage to ask whether we are innocent or guilty. The garden of innocence is a pre-human condition. When we question the extent of our guilt we are in a position to assess our own power and move beyond infantile dependency. Acknowledgment of guilt makes me an agent rather than a victim. I am potent. I caused certain events which led to certain consequences—some of which were injurious to others. I did it. Acknowledgment of guilt is a more advanced stage of individuation than living in the encompassing fog of shame.

And if there is guilt, the question of forgiveness is raised. Can I be forgiven? Can I begin again? If I am responsible for acts I committed in the past, then I have the power to act differently in the future. If I am not a responsible agent, then all I can do is grieve my past fate and succumb to whatever the future brings. Where there is no guilt-forgiveness-action, there is no longer any responsible person.

Our dignity is not in innocence but in guilt-forgiveness and new beginnings. I believe the most potent action comes from those persons who have been scarred and healed a thousand times. We act not as innocent children of the cosmos but as historical persons who have become gnarled and seasoned.

THE TYRANNY GAME
or
GOOD-BYE BIG DADDY

Introduction. My father is dead. But I have not entirely ceased to long for a benevolent and wise authority who will reveal the laws of reality and tell me what I must do to gain eternal life, achieve satori, or prevent premature senility. Within my psychic repertoire there is a frightened child who longs to be dominated, as well as a fascist dictator who loves to dominate others. My struggle with authority has centered on discovering what I may reasonably believe about life, what limits I choose for myself and what form of power I wish to exercise. I took the occasion of an Esalen conference on Spiritual and Therapeutic Tyranny to define my current relationship to the kind of authority I once found incarnate in my father.

The stage was set for high comedy. My assigned task was to pin the tail on some paper tigers, to challenge the new authorities in psychology and religion, to see whether the emperors of the new consciousness were wearing anything beneath their robes. The audience was filled with gurus (all male), irate women who saw the dominant male presence as the *prima facie* evidence of tyranny, and followers of several new messiahs anxious to proclaim the truth. As an authority I had to stand before many people who had been authorities for me and question the whole principle of authority. I was as nervous as if I had been challenging my father to a shootout at the I'm O.K. Corral. It was something of a coming-of-age ceremony for me.

Tyranny: absolute government in which power is vested in a single ruler . . . rigorous, cruel, oppressive and unjustly severe government whether by a single absolute ruler or other controlling power.

We enjoy the luxury of speaking openly about tyranny because we have so little of it. We are free to shout about repression because we are not repressed. Tyranny means armed guards, terror, torture and death for the opponents of the ruling authorities. It means that freedom of speech, of assembly, of protest may have to be paid for with blood. We are not without tyranny in this country but it exists as a scab on the surface of a still somewhat democratic society. It is not our interest here to establish some index by which we could judge how much or how little *political* tyranny exists within our country at the moment. That is an interesting and important question; it is not the one we are primarily concerned with. We are to look at the more subtle forms of tyranny that exist within the ambiance of therapists, healers, gurus and other professional spiritual guides. We are interested in seeing whether there is corruption within our own house rather than looking for termites in the Pentagon, or chauvinism in the establishment. Our concern is not so much what *they* do to *us* as what we do to ourselves, our *freely chosen bondage* —voluntary submission.

Tyranny as metaphor.
Fascism as analogy.
We are just playing;
looking for the rules
of the game.

The metaphor is political;
it's a matter of governance

of the body politic
or the body.
Who controls the wealth
or the commonwealth?
Who leads the group
and who is lead?
The use and abuse of power.
Who has dominion over the people?
All power to . . . ?

What rules govern the game?
What are the regulation moves when we play:
Lord and liege
Master and slave
Guru and disciple
Therapist and client
Leader and follower
Enlightened and seeker?

Tyranny is:
law and order gone wild,
an inordinancy in the body politic,
a cancer in the organism.
A part seizes control over the whole.
There is an epileptic seizure of power
and the head is cut off from the body.
Spiritual capitalism; everything is ruled
    from above.
The elite meet and decide how the mass is
    to be governed.
The chosen ones, the enlightened, the
    guardians, the shamen, the priests,
the natural leaders, the gurus, the tulkus,
    the philosophers, the therapists, the
    strong men and liberated women—all
    those with brighter minds and higher

consciousnesses in whose ears god has
whispered the secrets of human nature
and has shown visions of the ideal—become
the architects of a new humanity and a new
utopia.

(Should we mention in passing that the leaders are
usually male, privileged, articulate, more comely than
average, up-tight, and are often more successful in public
than private? No. Let's not mention that.)

And the leaders always, in theory and rhetoric, accept
power for the sake of the masses. It is for your own good,
you know. The body can't be expected to mind itself. The
children are innocent and weak; they are still asleep
dreaming in the world of maya, playing with their illusions.
They don't have access to the information necessary
to make policy decisions. They haven't seen the archetypes. They are not enlightened. They still have egos. They
need help.

The FIRST RULE of the game is: *It takes two to play.*
There must be the will to dominate and the will to submit.
You can't play follow the leader without an agreement.
In this game there are no innocent parties . . .

Cops and robbers. Guards and inmates. I took a tour
of Alcatraz. When I saw the cells and the dark isolation rooms I hated the guards. How could those
bastards have administered such brutalizing punish-
ment to their fellows. Then I thought how hard an
inmate had to work at it to end up in Alcatraz. You
had to be bad and badder until you proved you were
the baddest-ass around. Then you got the prize—the
rock, the most repressive prison in the system. The
game was brutal, but guards and inmates together
set up the checker board.

Therapists require patients—and vice versa
Disciples require gurus—and versa vice

The SECOND RULE: *the game begins in the mud.* If there is no one who is diseased there is no need for a healer. So we begin with mental illness, neurosis, alienation, sin, behavioral difficulties, insanity or some such negative condition that is to be corrected. Those who are to play the part of patient or disciple must feel that they are somehow less than human, less than adequate.

The play begins with a confession:

> We have all sinned and fallen short of the glory of god or the human potential or the expectations of our sisters. We have repressed our natural sexuality and our libidos have been driven deep underground. Our egos are inflated and we have not wakened from illusions. We live at minus satori levels. We still have attachments and of course we are all chauvinistic, and also a little passive-dependent. We are not very loving and we try too hard to please. We don't cope very well or take total responsibility for our actions. We are racists, classists, sexists and we are getting flabby around the erogenous zones.

The THIRD rule is: *The patient-client-disciple must be taught the rules of the game to which he is to submit if he is to be freed of his dis/ease and catch the prize of happiness.* The rules are always conditional.

If you will:
    repent of your sin
    free associate
    give up your attachments
    reduce your ego
    have faith in . . .
    lose your mind and come to your senses

strengthen your ego and control your infantile emotions
release your engrams
give up your defense mechanisms
soften your character armor
let out a primal scream
meditate on your mantra
accept the perfect master
overthrow the repressors
take total responsibility for your self
follow the leader

then you will . . . (Here comes the promise.
Promise them everything,
but give them . . .

The FOURTH RULE is: *Set the goal of human life so high that no one can attain it.* Otherwise the game would end. The ideal must be unattainable, it must always recede just when you were about to catch it.)

then you will . . .
receive grace
make your unconscious conscious and
be freed from the irrational
love freely with no fear of loss and
no hint of jealousy
merge with the cosmic one
live in the kingdom of the here and now
be satisfied with reality
be clear
be open
have the perfect orgasm
be cured of neurosis
find peace of mind
discover the true path

live in an erotic utopia
transcend the barriers which keep you
from having life go exactly the way
  you want it to go
realize the human potential
enter into the dictatorship of the pro-
  letariat
enjoy polymorphous perversity
remain in satori 24
reach nirvana
reconcile the contradictions
trade in all those brown stamps at
  the Redemption center and buy
  yourself a little bit a heaven. *Amen!*

The End. The Apocalypse. The Goal is reached. We got there. The game is finished. The kingdom of completion arrived right on schedule and we all lived happily ever after. At least that is how the game was supposed to end.

One small problem. (Remember they promise you—everything. But you only get a sniff of Arpège.) Maybe there were a few perfect moments, a little more peace, some clarity, a hint of metaphysical relaxation, times of liberation. But nothing like the big bang; no permanent satori 24. Dis-illusioned. Now what can we do? We can try harder or switch messiahs or quit the game.

Californians have a special constitutional weakness for new messiahs:

Zen in the 50s
LSD in the 60s
Encounter and sensitivity
New left visions
Arica
est
etc.

But tomorrow never comes. The kingdom of Ends is not of this world. When I was thirteen with one wild hair I knew beyond a shadow of a doubt that Jesus would come again and usher in the Millenium. I longed for the age beyond ambiguity. But I prayed that Jesus would wait until I lost my virginity. My prayers were answered and since that day it has been hard for me to believe in the second coming. But I never quite stopped hoping to surrender dominion over my life to some strange Lord or Lady. Even after psychoanalysis, encounter, rolfing, gestalt and a few others that didn't usher in the end of time I find I am still a sucker for the game. I'll play either part—heads or tails, guru or disciple—so long as I don't have to quit the game entirely. Tell me about a new wise man from the East and for a while I will wonder if, perhaps, he has the answer.

If the promise is not fulfilled why does the game go on?

The FIFTH RULE is: *The payoff of the game is the illusion of power.* Both players in the tyranny game win because they get to remain in the ambiance of power. It's a power-game: Let's pretend human beings have the power to control life. It doesn't matter whether you are the dominator or the dominated because both parties share the same illusion. So long as they remain hypnotized by the power game men and women are able to avert their faces from the terrifying impotence of the human condition. At any moment death or catastrophe can wipe away all we cherish and have worked so hard to make secure. No human power can make life secure. But since this is such a terrifying fact we find ways to preserve the illusion that someone can control our destiny.

There is a way to end the game that can't be won.
If we see where and why it began.

THE ROOTS OF TYRANNY

Full blown the game sounds grim:

> dominate or submit
> control or be controlled
> be the wolf or be the hare
> one up or one down
> be the pig or do the jig
> sad-ism or mass-ochism.

But it all began in so small and human a way. Every vice is only a virtue gone to seed. We all entered this world of giants and gods as squirming six pound, fifteen-inch midgets. They were big and we were small and there was comfort and security in the unequal world. And for a lifetime the play between big and small will go on within each of us.

Last year I returned to a childhood home in Tennessee and went to visit an old lady who had loved and cared for the Keen children as if they were her own. Miss Inny was the only Quaker in East Tennessee and she was tart and bittersweet as a muscadine grape. She would spit in the eyes of a sheriff or a college president and bake biscuits for hungry children. For over 30 years she had been taking care of her bedridden sister—now ninety years old. Miss Evie was completely paralyzed and could "talk" to Inny only by winking her eyes. But right before she had the stroke which took her speech away she woke one night and called out for Inny. "We have to get up and go to the old house and clean it up and cook some chicken and biscuits for Mother. Oh, I'm so glad Mother is coming." Inny convinced her to wait till morning. By that time the dream had passed. As she told me about it Inny started crying,

"Sammy, Sammy, can you imagine a ninety-year-old woman still calling out in the night for her mother?"

And I started crying. Because I could. I thought of my father—nine years dead—and remembered how warm and friendly the nights of childhood were because his booming voice could hold all the hounds of hell at bay and chase away the spirits that ruled the darkness. Father, Father, who does not want a strong and wise protector? Who is so grown up as to have lost the desire for protection against the terrors of the night? The beasties and things that go bump don't wear the faces of bears or burglars as we get older. They all begin to wear the mask of death. And in the presence of that old man we are all small and impotent and we flock to Master-Father-Guru-God who promises us protection.

> So the search begins for a new Father.
> Let's pretend you are wise and strong
>   and I am your little child.
> But for most of us the game gets old.
> The best therapist turns out to have
> a clay heart.
> And Fritz was a nasty old man
> And Maharaji has ulcers
> And Freud couldn't give up cigars
> And Bill Schutz doesn't jump for joy
> And Ida needs rolfing
> And Tillich was a swinger
> And John Lilly has migraines in his
> tape loops.
> And the President was a criminal
> And Sam Keen can't dance
> And it is probable that
> Mike Murphy plays only average golf
> And Dear Abby keeps a
> lover on the side.

God is dead
The authorities just lost the ball on the
five-yard line.
Our turn now.
The kingdom, and the power and the glory
are ours.
Time to change sides.
We get to become the Fathers, the Giants.
And once we have the power we will be as
careful and careless as they.
We will pretend certainty because the
smaller ones who depend on us require security.
We will pretend to have banished death
because they demand immortality.
We will be heroes because life without
glory is unbearable.
We will manage, control and set limits
because we are good parents.
We will help and nourish because young
life needs care.

After we have played both parts in the game the crucial moment comes when we have the chance to end the game —to play the end-game. Whether a parent or a therapist is a good or a bad giant depends on whether he will play the end-game when the time comes.

A good therapist, a wise giant, watches the little ones growing larger and chuckles as they get nearer the point where they will unmask his pretentions, when they will seize the kingdom and the power for themselves.

The good giant is a trickster, a koan, a screen on which the small ones project their power until they are ready to claim it for themselves.

A Zen Tale: A young man came to a master seeking enlightenment.

"Master, show me the way to enlightenment," he said.
"Kill me," the master replied.

  The end-game. The players change sides
and we all sit down and laugh together:
the Giants never had any power that was
not ours.

Now the game is really over.
No more big and small, I'm up and you're down.
No more Fathers and Mothers (with capital
letters)
We found the divine virtue hidden in the
vice of domination and submission.
We each need to care and be cared for,
to exercise and respect power.
We have played the end-game
  and now we can begin the most exciting
  game of all:
  It is called: *Equality*
  And that one doesn't end,
  because it takes a lifetime
  to learn to play it well.

It is so human a thing to play
big and small
follow the leader.
The chasm over the void of death is deep
and the tightrope we have
to walk is precarious.
The line is hard to draw between
tyranny and discipline
submission and surrender
hope and utopia
nurturing and smothering
helping and crippling
depending and dependency

faith and credulity
reason and rationalization
acceptance and resignation
compromise and betrayal.

I find I am continually seduced back into
the tyranny game. And now I can play either
part with equal facility.

One of my protections is an *anti-tyranny*
kit I keep to remind me who I am. It is
filled with yes's and no's and some maybe's,
things I believe and don't believe.

ANTI-TYRANNY KIT

No!

I do not believe in the Grand Inquisitor.

When I am tired I want miracle, mystery and authority as much as the next person but the price is too high.
I love cosmic security but Big Daddy always wants my
freedom in exchange. I would rather believe in my
own potency some of the time than be assured of His
all of the time. Submission is sweet—we all have a
chapter in our autobiographies called *The Story of O.*
—but freedom is sweeter. With all of its terror it is
better to live in the wilderness than the ant heap. I
don't have any confidence that the spiritual elite—
god's mafia—will awaken and save the nation and
show us the true way. Democracy is hazardous, but
it is the best risk we have.

I do not believe in getting it all together.

The self cannot be unified. We are schizophrenics by
nature. Spontaneity and self-consciousness do the

tango within us so long as we remain conscious animals. We are amphibians living in the tooth and claw of nature and in the care-full-ness of community. Our schizophrenia is our glory, the token of our humanness.

I do not believe in a life without attachments.

Those without attachments are free to be tyrannized, to be totally attached to the leader's trip. We love children and friends and places and things because we are specific human beings. Maybe God loves everyone equally, or not at all, but the human kind are attached and partisan and beautifully contorted in their loves. To be human means keeping at least one foot firmly rooted in Boaz, Alabama, or some such improbable point of incarnation.

I do not believe in telling all my secrets.

I don't believe in complete openness, transparence, keeping an open house in my soul, a life without defense mechanisms. Private space, secrecy, is necessary and it is a mystery that should not be profaned. If I invite you in it will be because you are special to me, and I trust you will treasure the intimacy and friendship more for knowing it is not instant and is not offered indiscriminately. To be me I must discriminate and include some and exclude others from the circle of caring.

I do not believe in speed.

It takes a lifetime to live a life, and the instant cures— weekend escalators to satori—are nostrums which keep alive the hopes for permanent and easy solutions.

I do not believe in reincarnated beings

Primal screams that drain the pool of pain
realizing the human potential
the perfectly rolfed body
perfect marriages
perfect masters
(I can't even find the
perfect pair of shoes.)

Yes!

I believe in permanent imperfection.

Satori O. Samsara is nirvana. So long as we are alive we will be moved by dreams that are real but may never be actual. Our home is on the road. The human animal is hungry and can never be wholly satisfied. Avoid those who want to fill the void. The emptiness is necessary. The most reliable contentment comes from knowing we will never be finished, exhausted, used up. I am not yet: therefore I hope.

I believe in Endarkenment.

The part is ignorant of the whole. The human condition is one of selective ignorance. We see little and it is always distorted by who we are. The distortion is called art. No one of us is the center of the universe, but each of us sees things as if they all revolved around him or her. It is folly to believe we can see from everywhere or nowhere. We filter all knowledge through our autobiographies.

I believe in Death.

Because it is more certain than all the theories which invite us to disbelieve in it. And because so long as we evade the fear of coming to an end we never begin or begin again.

I believe in the ego.

Because it is my playmate and the game would forfeit if it left me altogether. This strange entity I am has a history and a name—I am called Sam Keen. Whatever is universal, cosmic and beyond time within me is always homogenized with the ego, the identity, the continuity, the story I call myself. I blend and lose my boundaries in dreams, in love, in play, in those delightful moments of self-forgetfulness but in the evening I always come home to the hearth of my self-consciousness. Rather than ridding myself of my ego I would like to appreciate it more, applaud my own drama more wholeheartedly.

I believe in Time.

Life is the teacher and the years are the path. The major discipline is negotiating those turbulent passages that seem to come every ten years or so. The task of making the young into prematurely peaceful beings is comical. Wisdom is a vice at twenty and a necessity at sixty. There is a time for adolescent insanity and the folly of second childhood, and a time for planning, renunciation and work. Most of what we call happiness is only a matter of knowing what time it is and not taking clues from anyone else's clock.

I believe in Friendship.

Dad and Mother, Lawrence, Ruth Ann, Jackie, Heather, Jane, Lael, Gif, Howard, Michael, Anne, Eliza, Linnea, Jim, Jan, Jerry and others. Because I care for them and they care for me and care always smells like an unmistakable person. And because I don't know anything higher than friendship.

I believe in Hope.

Because the universe is open and I don't know what may happen and the realest things turn out to be unreal and vice versa. And I can't figure out what this crazy drama is about so I may as well trust it is about something good.

I believe Life can't be tamed or controlled.

When I was sixteen years old, and possessed of more answers and less experience than I now have, I wanted with all my wanting to be a rancher. I reverenced everything that smelled of horse or saddle leather. One shrine I visited regularly was a small corral at the back of a donut shop on the Philadelphia Pike in Wilmington, Delaware—an improbable place for an epiphany. A stallion lived there in an enclosure hardly large enough for a backyard barbecue. Most afternoons after school I went to visit him. He must have been seventeen-hands high—chestnut colored with a wide blaze in the middle of his nose. His muscles danced wildly inside a shining coat. He was, altogether, a horse fit for a minor divinity to ride into battle. Once when his owner allowed a friend to take him out of the corral I got to ride him in a large field

41

down by the river. It was like all the outlaws in all the movies riding toward freedom. That is, until he sniffed a mare in some unknown pasture and took off like hell. The owner finally had to rescue both of us, and he returned my friend to prison and was none too happy with me for not being able to control the stallion. Not long after the owner decided the horse would have to be gelded. He wasn't safe to keep in suburbia. And he asked me if I would come on the following Saturday to help the veterinarian with the job.

> Do you leave your god to suffer alone
> Or share his pain?

For some reason that took half a lifetime to understand, I went. The veterinarian arrived, gave the necessary shots to deaden the consciousness and the pain. The stallion was eased off his feet and rested on the ground. The incisions were made. The testicles with their long roots reaching up into the fire in the stomach were removed. The wound cauterized. And the stunned horse struggled to his feet.

I vomited.

I suppose he was gentle afterwards and could be ridden. I never went to visit him again.

I wish I had not shared in the violation of that Saturday morning. It seems better to fail a hundred times, to be thrown time and again to the ground than to tame the wild god.

BROKEN MATRIX

"The world begins to exist when the individual discovers it. He discovers it when he sacrifices the "mother," when he has freed himself from the mists of his unconscious conditions within the mother."

—CARL JUNG

From California through "the friendly skies of United" (served by plastic girls who might if you asked but would smell of Arrid), I come East toward what was once home. A migratory bird returning to a now barren turf driven by the instinctual dream of nurture and safe nesting. Soon I must come to ground. For the moment I float in the airborne womb that bears me through timeless space. Before landing there is time for drifting, for indecision, for ambivalence. And wondering: Where is home? What may I claim of the past? How free am I to allow my future to be born out of my present desires rather than out of my childhood fears?

Landing. ("Please remain in your seat until the aircraft has reached the terminal. . . . ") I reset my watch. Three hours lost in transit. Time is already out of sorts with the rhythms of my body. Dreamlike I move through the interstices between the worlds—carpeted lounges, tiled corridors, escalators (which, unlike history, move automatically toward a predestined end), freeways—through the gray smogset toward the street, the house, the place that was the matrix of my becoming.

The porch creaks under my step as I advance toward the inner sanctum. There are doors to be opened. Always, more doors than necessary. First I must observe the ritual opening of the storm door. Its aluminum frame yawns, ludicrously empty of all glass that might protect the inner world from the winds of winter. I pass beyond the second door into the hallway. Mother waits. We walk toward each other as if we might embrace, but taut threads of reserve hold us apart. I kiss her on the cheek (and wonder whether betrayal is a willful form of frozen passion).

I sink down into the couch ("Sit up straight. Keep your shoulders high" . . . "To hell with it. I like slouching").

"Would you like some coffee and cookies?"

"Sure." (A little caffeine to stimulate the nerves and something sweet to bolster the blood sugar. They might counteract the lassitude that swallows me in this place.)

The antiphonal liturgy for infrequent meetings begins.

"How are you?"

"Fine. How are you?"

"O.K. I can't complain. (I hurt.) It has been a hard year but everything is going well now. I am finally getting back to my writing. (Keep it vague. She would be disturbed if she knew what I was writing.) What's new around here?"

"Nothing much. (His face looks strained. Why doesn't he relax and stop fighting with himself?) I got the roof repaired and the new tile on the bathroom. Next week I am going . . ."

The phone rings. I answer it. A racked, halting voice of some ancient crone asks for Ruth.

"It's for you, Mother. It sounds like an echo from the morgue."

"That will be Margaret. She is paralyzed and can hardly talk. . . . Hello, Margaret. . . . I'll be glad to. Just tell me what you want. . . . Two fish sticks. The ones on sale or the regular ones? . . . One banana. I don't think I can get a pint of milk. Will a quart be all right? . . . O.K. I'll try to get it for you tomorrow morning . . . Oh, it's all right. I don't mind. Good-by."

"It sounds like you are still taking care of all the lame ducks in town (Why can't she be more accepting of me?)."

"Not all of them, but quite a few . . . How are Lael and Gifford? (I know they are terribly hurt by this whole mess.)"

"They are fine. (I know she doesn't believe me.) I talk to them on the phone every night, and they visit me in California every few weeks. In some ways I am closer to them than I was before. Now that they are not with me, I realize how much I love them."

For a moment our talk totters on the edge of meeting. Then we retreat into the unasked questions and unspoken judgments. Sentences are spoken but not joined. Talk and silence alternate in an awkward dance.

Supper is served (Swiss steak. She always remembers what I like to eat). I settle into an agitated silence. A thick crust of passivity covers the void of frustration. The movements of the evening are like an underwater ballet—slow, deliberate and indistinct.

In the hermetic theaters of our minds solitary monologues are formed. Clairvoyants, joined forever in the womb-world, know in the silence each long-guarded secret. We have heard more clearly than words what has never been said:

I'm forty years old and still a son. In spite of the shame I still want your face to shine upon me and your eyes to delight in my presence. I crave your approval. Like an addict I have traveled through what has never been quite the world searching for something you never gave me. Or I never accepted. And fame has been no more gentle, for public eyes are not green like yours.

His hawk eyes are always searching, analyzing and judging me. I know I failed, tried too hard to make him into my own image of a Christian, didn't enjoy him enough for just being himself. But I was troubled with myself then, and busy raising five children and taking care of the business. But that is all past. I wish he would accept me as I am and relax with himself.

Through the touchless hours of punctuated silence my body grows old and heavy with despair. As the dissonance increases I know I must break the taboo, I must dip into the well of unspoken knowledge we share.

"Mother, I have to talk to you. We have a habit of never

saying the important things. So I visit you but we never meet. If we can't talk as adults, as people who still have something to say to one another, what is the use of going through these pantomimes of meeting?"

"What do you want from me?"

"I'm not sure. I guess I still want your approval. I want you to be pleased with me."

"How can I be pleased when I see you in pain? I see you destroying yourself. You turn all of your intensity inward and try to make yourself into some image you have of yourself. I know you are sincere but . . ."

"I'm misguided! I'm wrong! That's it, isn't it?"

"Sam, I don't mean to judge, but I see you breaking God's laws and I know only unhappiness can come of it."

"You mean the divorce?"

"Yes."

"We are doing what seems best to us. We have come to the end of the time when it seems good for us to be together. We want different things in life, and so the paths that ran together for so many years now have to separate. There is a lot of grief involved. But I don't think we have betrayed each other."

"But you are tearing yourself up. And the children."

"There are worse things than pain. The deadness and hostility that came before were far more destructive than the grief."

"But you have responsibilities. You took vows and made promises before God. Doesn't that mean anything to you?"

"Certainly. But I don't know how to think about vows and promises anymore. I thought they were forever. Now it seems the best thing Heather and I can do is to release each other and separate."

"That doesn't make any sense to me. Sometimes I think the whole world has gone crazy. Whatever happened to duty and responsibility and morality? You don't quit when the going gets hard. I can't help it. I can't see it any other way. What you are doing is adultery. And it is clearly contrary to God's law and can only bring you unhappiness."

"That's your judgment. It is against the will of *your* God. Not mine. This is where we always miss each other. You think God has some plan for my life and you know it better than I. You don't respect the integrity of the way I move through my own life."

"Do you respect my way? Don't you think I am just a simple-minded old woman whose religion is a crutch, a kind of quaint myth? You have always been critical of my beliefs because they were too simple."

"It's true. I have. I always wanted to enlighten you. But I have given up the job. I think your way is right for you. But what has been a way of life for you was a way of death for me."

"You haven't tried it."

"That's a lie. A goddamn lie. And you know it. (Don't talk that way to your Mother!) For years I tried to mold myself to your image of a Christian. I prayed and read the Bible. I tried to believe all the essentials of the faith. Whenever doubts crept into my mind I tried to purge them until I was half crazy with the split between what I had to believe to have your approval and what I had to believe if I was going to trust my experience. For God's sake, I was twenty-two years old before I made the decision to trust my own mind. And only now, at forty, have I decided to trust my body. The only way I know is trusting the promptings of my deepest self. So don't ever say I rejected your way without trying it. I won't sit still and let you say that."

"You don't have to get angry and shout at me."

"Yes I do. If I am going to talk to you. I am mad now and I won't pretend otherwise."

"Well, I don't like it."

"I know that. You and Granny always wanted me to be a gentle-man. Well, I'm only half gentle. The rest of me is mad and angry and crazy and wild and I don't want to be tamed."

"There doesn't seem to be much danger of that."

"Ha. Most everything in modern life is a conspiracy to tone people down and make them bland."

"You take yourself so seriously. Why can't you get out of yourself? Let God be your savior and take the burden of your self away."

"You make it sound so easy. Just surrender your self. I have to start with my self. If I can't trust myself I can't trust the world. I know the disgust of being trapped in my ego. But I also know something of the rare joy of forgetting myself. Besides, you were the one who taught me to insist upon my own path. You always insisted that I know for myself, that I find my own truth. But you rejected me when the truth I found was different from your truth."

"No, Sam. No. Not rejected you. I never rejected you. I know you think that but it's not true. I've always had a hard time demonstrating affection. I was taught as a child to be reserved, and I've never been able to break through that. But I have always loved you. (Tears, soft and with dignity, seep through her—my Mother's—restraint.) It's just that I have always wanted the best for you, and you seem to have struggled so much and had so little peace."

Silence.

Tears, soft and with dignity, seep through my—her son's—restraint. Something in me dissolves. It is as if constricted blood vessels running up and down my left side suddenly are connected with my heart, and blood flows through them. I look and MOTHER is no longer there. The goddess Maya, the source and validation of my being has disappeared. The giantess who might give all gifts but chooses to withhold is gone. In her place my mother, Ruth McMurray Keen, sixty-three, rich as good earth. As sudden as revelation, I see the struggle of her life, her strength and her integrity, and I know how privileged I am to have been born of fiery parents, fierce in their beliefs and inhabited by strong virtues. I recognize my mother.

Silence.

Our reserve, like frost turning autumn leaves into riotous fall, comes back into the room. And we welcome it like an old friend.

"Well, Mother, I guess we will just have to live with each other's fanaticism. I suppose the same God rules our separate worlds."

"I guess so."

We look at each other, familial strangers, blooded together beyond separation by memories and hopes of many lifetimes. There will be no agreement between us, nor any betrayal.

I return to my room but cannot sleep. Now I am alone without the protecting gods. Stunned by the sudden knowledge of my loneliness, I wander in the labyrinthine memories of childhood searching for a way into the light of the present. In the corner of my room is a box of old photographs. I bring it to the desk and sort through the pictures and place the generations in order:

Grandmother McMurray holding Ruth McMurray. Age one.

Grandfather McMurray looking (gentle and reserved), at Grandmother McMurray (I wonder if they ever made love in the woods and played afterwards in a stream?).

Grandmother and Grandfather Keen (looking like nothing gentler and less utilitarian than a brick building in the industrial section of Wilmington, Delaware, that housed Keen's Dried Beef).

Ruth McMurray Keen (Age nineteen. Cameo bride in white. Looking like the dark and mysterious archetype of woman. I never liked blonds).

J. Alvin Keen (Age middle-twenties. Dark and dashing. Black eyes that shone of innocence and potential violence. Looking sometimes like Douglas Fairbanks, sometimes like a hit-man for the mafia).

Lawrence Keen and Sam Keen (Ages ten and eight. Lawrence holding a dirigible built from an erector set and I in my Royal Canadian Mounted Police uniform. He always wanted to put things together with his hands, and I wanted to know about the disguises, the masks and what was beneath them. We are both interested in how things work).

Ruth Ann and Jackie (Ages 8 and 6. In dress-up gowns of egg-shell satin made by Granny for little ladies. Already Jackie's golden curls are a crown to her talkative charm. We are alike. Ruth Ann is silent, in the background, like Lawrence, very reserved).

Sam, Lawrence, Dad. 1941. Fishing trip. Miami, Florida. (How many eons and worlds ago. I was then the age my son Gif is now. How can I bear to live apart from him? Fathers are such gods to their sons. The twilight of the gods: the absence of the fathers.)

1954. Wedding pictures. Sam and Heather. (Pencil thin and fragile in a world we knew would be orderly and continuous with the time before. Secure in our knowledge that we were mating for better or worse until . . . death.)

Christmas, 1962. The whole family together. The gathering of the clan. Three generations. No one is missing. (But death is already whispering in the barren trees. Sol Invictus. The birth of the Sun. Birth and death of the son. After the death of the father the birth of the son . . . Did you have to die for me to live? Could we not have shared the kingdom, the power and the glory?)

Christmas, 1970. Sam, Heather, Lael, Gifford. On the surface all is calm. The continuity seems secure. (Under the surface . . .)

I sit before the generations in silence. The pictures blur and flow together like rain falling into a grey December sea. Crying softly. Overwhelmed by the sorrow of transcience. In the passing of time I had hoped for a familiar thread to wind throughout my days. Now the thread is broken. Divorce, discontinuity. Who will know how the chapters of life fit together? Who will tell my story?

Doubt weaves its way between the grief and the loneliness of the night. Being alone, there is no barrier against the skepticism that believes only in what has already been. The voices begin to haunt me: "Only a fool believes in life after forty. It is too late to begin again. You are what you have been. Your patterns of happiness are already programmed into the tissue of your mind and body. Your history is your destiny. Don't fight against it. Rebirth is an illusion. There is a single path upon which a man may walk without courting destruction. Go back. Go back. Go back to the fork in the road and continue on your original way."

Panic seizes me and the voices within shout at each other.

There is only one way. And you have lost it. God has a plan for your life and you are missing it. Surrender your pride and your intensity and your effort to control your life. Your path is predestined. Accept it or die.

Goddamn you, John Calvin. You prison keeper. Jailer to the generations of the earnest. You enemy of the joyful body. I hate your goddamn rational, constipated god who still rules the industrial world with WASPish cruelty.

I am again in the grip of the demoness. Kali. Mother

Goddess, creator and destroyer. I feel myself being sucked down into an encompassing matrix, into the womb of the single world where all must be explained, understood. I am being seduced by the appeal of security. The sirens' voices invite me to surrender to the single path and promise a tranquilized happiness. With fascinated horror I watch myself being wrapped in the cosmic maternal web, imprisoned by the fears of the unknown plural world and stung into immobility and insensitivity.

Finally sleep comes. And with it healing dreams.

Dream fragment. I have two guitars, curvaceous, lovely to touch, capable of playing the songs that are in me. But I cannot play the new guitar until the old one burns and is destroyed.

In half-sleep I allow my dream to speak to me: Consume your past. Do not preserve it. "The new comes not out of the old but out of the death of the old." (Tillich—you wise old fox. You knew. You took the journey.) Conversion: turning around, facing the world rather than the past. He who would enter the kingdom of the present must kill his father and mother. Divorce, discontinuity. No rebirth without trauma. It is impossible to know before it happens. Resurrection seems an insane dream—until it happens. Hope means escape from the sanctuary of the already determined world of the mothered-and-fathered past.

Waking. Swimming up to the world of casual clarity. The possession is growing weaker. The cacophony within is lessening. The sanity necessary to live in the wild world is returning. In medieval times the sign of the cross was reputed to chase away evil spirits and break the spell of demons. I wish there was some sign I could make to dispel the Christian-mother-goddess who at times has me in her presence. With what may I conjure? The new reality is vague and savory. It does not have the clarity of abstraction. Freedom is in dissolution of forms. Knowing is in uncertainty. My passage has been from illusions of certainty to the certainty of illusions—marvelous dis-illusionment. My former knowledge was only a defense against ignorance, a barrier erected against the threat of the unknown. And my morality was baptized fear. The touchstones of the new reality are few. (Image: Jumping across a stream from stone to stone. I get my feet wet. The stones are not a bridge. But they allow me to cross over the river.) What sign will dispel the reasonable madness of a securely ordered world? Only flesh can break the captivation of abstraction.

Pictures, scenes, smells, tastes from recent days invade me: An irregular black and white stone lying on the sand, bathed in the topaz light of the declining sun; the blended aroma of man and woman rising from love-warmed sheets; the rippling intensity of voices woven together in conversation; the sweet fatigue of a well-worked body; red wine and peanut butter spread thick on coarse wheat bread; my mother weeping, reserves of love flooding out to wear away old resentments.

I hold these fragments against the bewitchments of certainty. And gradually trust grows strong once again. I know they will carry me safely away from the broken matrix of my childhood dreams. I will move once again through the concrete, steel and plastic interstices and Trans World Airlines, and I will race the sun westward through the now disunited skies till it sinks into the terrible sea that lies quiet as a kitten on the doorstep of my new home.

3

The Empty Center

When the tides are changing there is a moment when the water is still.

Between
who you were
and might yet be
an interstice
a vacuum
nothing at all
except a chance
to begin again.

January 4, 1973. According to all the occult prophets there was supposed to be an earthquake today and California was to fall into the sea. I also have been expecting a cataclysm, a definite division between the continents of what I was and what I might yet be; an end to the old and a beginning of the new. Old fears are weaker but still present. My memory holds fast to all I have loved. No

54

earthquake today. But the hard edges of my resolve and
the clear outlines of my hopes are melting. Ebb tide. Nothing strong or decisive stirring. I am sucked into the vortex
of boredom. I am tempted to prod myself into action.
Violence is easier to bear than nothingness. I wanted to be
a rock in a river, splitting the water. Instead I seem to be a
fish finning my way through currents in a sea I cannot
control. How long will this fallowness, this dissolution last?
A week? A year? How long do I have to be wishy-washy?
Does my contract with life include an emergency clause
or a guarantee against earthquakes that don't happen?

Beneath anything no thing
Beneath words silence
Beneath strife calm
Beneath tension softness
Beneath life death.
And vice versa.

God must like empty spaces
He made a lot of nothing
That yearns to be filled
With something.

When I insist on wholes I turn the world into a goose-
stepping system of closed concepts and dogmatic explanations. Pay attention to the holes. It is in the empty
spaces—lacunae, vacuums, interstices, pauses, voids,
black holes in space—that new things begin. Creativity is
born from silence. Novelty comes from the unexplored
spaces, the badlands, the outlaw territory.

When I am whole, together, contained
nothing can get in.
The hole in the ego
is where the holy
flows in and out.

Broken
open
to the world.

Walking on the beach
looking for perfect shells.
I almost did not see
the intricate patterns
and broken beauty
of the fragments.

No/thing is holy.
Everything is.

God is said to have created the world *ex nihilo*
Why shouldn't we create ourselves out of the same
nothing?

We are always acting but sometimes the act is painful
and sometimes it is fun. To be human is to stage your own
drama. The point is not to look for an un-self-conscious
life of complete spontaneity. That is impossible. The trick
is to turn tragedy into comedy, to change the battlefield
into a playground.

What is the relation between the stage and the battle-field? During W. W. II we spoke about the European and the Pacific theaters. What is the hidden link between performance and violence? If we understood this we might be able to make our personal and political dramas more fun and more humane.

Here is one clue. When gorillas are threatened by invaders their first defense is a ritual act. They drum on their chests and make outlandish sounds. If their performance is successful violence is avoided. We perform because we are aware that our social reality depends upon the eyes of others. To be is to be seen. If we suspect that others are our enemies we put on a battlefield drama. But if we trust that the watching eyes are friendly we can do a little soft-shoe or comic routine. Most of the roles we play are motivated by fear. We pretend in order to disguise the fear; our centers are empty and *they* may find out. We pretend to hide the hole in the center.

But a wheel and a person must have a hole in the center in order to roll. The holy of holies is empty. Take away the predicates and you have the subject. The core of consciousness is empty. We can be filled with anything.

Keep running
chasing something
until you find nothing.
Those who run fastest
get nowhere first.
Their prize is defeat.

Nothing is so important as nothing.
Accept emptiness and you may be filled.

These are one and the same:
God
Nothing
Freedom
Void
Silence
The space between the synapses
The power to begin again.

Spring

*Ascent Toward
Light*

ne morning, just when it seemed the deadness of Winter would never pass, Person awoke unexpectedly to find green tendrils pushing up the lid of the Tomb of Nothingness. S/he felt the stirrings of New Life and decided to walk about and see what the World would look like now that the Old Authorities were dead.

Surprising things began to happen quite without Person's initiative or control. The New World seemed to reach out and welcome Person. Enchanted animals flocked around. Hawks and snakes came bearing Omens. There were dreams filled with messages, juicy as watermelons. Suddenly the World seemed to be a cypher, a hidden language of some Divine Presence, which Person knew made sense but could not quite understand. The Old World had been governed by Cause and Effect and other Laws written by the Society of Scientists, Moralists and Lawyers. But the New World was filled with Marvel and Synchronicity and as nearly as Person could determine seemed to be governed by a Council of Magicians, Comedians and Lovers. As Person continued the Journey there were stark peaks to be climbed and sparse deserts to be endured. But it seemed as if the path more frequently ran downhill than up, and as if a spring or oasis would appear just at the moment thirst became unbearable.

As the World seemed safer and more luscious Person became less of a Warrior and more of an Explorer. S/he shed much of the armor that encased the body and frequently went about naked and vulnerable. Gradually Person's body began to change. It became at once more feminine and more masculine, more tender and more fierce, more able to surrender to the rhythms and pulses of the day and to challenge and conquer obstacles along the way. It was as if Spirit and Flesh, which had always been hostile to each other in the Old World were suddenly reconciled. Head no longer tried to control Body.

As Person became more embodied in the New World Laughter broke through the defenses of Seriousness. The lines on Person's face that traced the history of Tragic Conflict began to soften and the smiles of Comedy began to appear.

And the light of Spring bathed the New World.

4

The Surprising New World

When the old self dies
a new world is born.

What was stale
is renewed by wonder.

The surprise
bursts out
of nothingness.

The young earth
is ruled by the unexpected.

Things will never be the same again.

THE OMENHAWK

In retrospect I see there were many clues that pointed
to the cataclysm that was to come. There were signs that
my old life was breaking apart and my world was to
undergo a radical change. The hawk was only the first
of the omens.

Let me begin, like a good scientist, with facts. In April of 1970 I was sitting in my office at the Center for Studies of the Person in downtown La Jolla. (Imagine: the pure light of Southern California, the sensual, antiseptic, electric-Day-Glo, modern world shorn of demons or holy places——California the mecca of the secular.) As I looked out of my window I saw a hawk (shall I pause, go to a book and check the species, perhaps the Latin name; shall I search out the universal category, discover the pedigree, to assure myself that my meeting with the strange one falls under the secure category of "knowledge"?) fly down and try to grab the narrow ridge of the prefabricated aluminum window frame. He missed. Tried again. On the third attempt (inferior helicopter) he made it. There he sat looking at me for eternal seconds. I, thinking only of a hawk sitting on a window ledge, was too sunk in curiosity to wonder, too caught by the peculiar appearance of a universal phenomenon to see the epiphany of the individual moment. Whether from the desire to share or to verify the experience I do not know, but I called my office-mate to look at the bird. But he (the bird—perhaps she) took off, circled the courtyard once and disappeared into the slightly smog-colored sky. And I, a single observer (insufficient for scientific purposes) was left with the story of an unrepeatable event.

Cut. Change scenes. Same day. The hour is late. The place: the long beach near Del Mar. A single layer of gauze is dropped between the observer and the scene to suggest a fragile fog that falls just before dark by the sea. A lone figure is climbing a cliff path which leads away from the beach. As he nears the top of the cliff three birds fly by silhouetted against the psychedelic sky.

And . . .

Suddenly . . .

I came awake with a start: the birds, the bird, the hawk,

THE HAWK. THE HAWK WAS AN (thoughts swirl so fast the sequence is lost; and in the confusion I waken to what I saw but did not see) OMEN. The hawk I had seen this morning (the distance between the subject and the object, the perception and the recognition, the phenomenon and the epiphany is the precise problem of the modern consciousness which must have problems without mysteries and facts without meanings) was an omen. Subject and predicate joined in matrimony to form a single fact in my mind—The Omenhawk.

Philosophical Parenthesis 1: Hard-headed Questions

No sooner was the romantic coupling celebrated than the critics of the mind entered to pull asunder what wondering perception had joined. Analysis, explanation and logic lined up rational objections by-the-numbers, slick as transistor circuits in IBM's or ICBM's:

1. We object to the marriage of the subject and the predicate as an incompatible joining of fact and fiction. There was a hawk. But no omen.

2. The time elapsed between the appearance of the hawk and the emergence of the conviction of the omen is *prima facie* evidence that the category of "omen" was grafted on to an event which has a purely naturalistic explanation.

3. The idea of "omens" is a superstition which is not acceptable to the "modern" mind (a category to watch). It went out when electricity and flush toilets came in.

4. The overplus of meaning suggested in "omenhawk" is a product of the symbolic faculty of the unconscious. The hawk (as symbol) was already

present in the psychological history of Sam Keen and the actual hawk only triggered a crystalization of insight whose components were present prior to the event. The magic is easily explained as a mistake in perception. The office-mate might have seen the hawk but not seen it as the omen.

5. Even *if* the hawk were an omen, how would anyone know its meaning? There are no guidelines for understanding a world in which omens occur.

Philosophical Parenthesis 2: Tender Hearted Questions

Once "if" (the bare possibility that "poetic fictions" might have ontological status) crept into the inner dialogue between the mystic and the analyst within my psyche, the questions I asked myself began to emerge out of some primal deep, some primitive place of trust, or credulity. I (a Harvard-educated ex-professor who knew the history, phenomenology and psychology of illusions and did not believe in omens) had been "visited." And I found myself asking: "I wonder what the 'omen' meant?"

What if: the primitive perspective is as true as the scientific perspective and the world is filled with signs, messages and miracles?

What if: everything addresses me—if I only have the eyes to see between the phenomena and the ears to listen to the silence?

What if: the space and time in which I live are tailored to my exact specifications?

What if: I (and every other person) am the exact center of a universe of meaningful events?

What if: everything that is purely natural is wholly magical?

What if: novelty is more fundamental than law?

Of course this is all foolishness. When we call some-one mad we mean he sees the world differently than the other voters. Sanity is the virtue of the masses. Those who are saved from simple sanity become fools. But if sanity locks us into a goose-stepping world of explanations, and laws, it might be worth the risk of foolishness to live in a free and surprising universe.

The most important question for me is not why I was unexpectedly visited by folly but why it took me so long to welcome it. How can I join the subject and the predicate together in shorter order (without a six-hour parenthesis between the event and unpack-ing the event of the meaning that was homogenized into it)? What kind of novacaine has modernity in-jected into my psychic nerve endings that has dead-ened me to the personal ways in which the universe addresses me?

What was the message the Omenhawk came to deliver? And who or what sent him?

I remain free as long as I can be surprised.

A free spirit needs the wilderness.

It keeps happening faster than I can record it. Just as I was about to write about the wilderness my son Gif came wheeling in on his bike—complete with "sissy bar" and ram's-horn handlebars slightly above eye level—and inter-rupted me. The wind at his back, the spirit in his eyes. "Dad, you'll never believe this. You think the wind is blowing hard here. Well, it's so strong over by Mark's house

that I had to pedal downhill. *Downhill!* It's unbelievable."
And it is. Until he is taught differently. Once he grows up
he will learn about laws and he will be able to calculate
the speed of the wind and divide by the angle of the grade
and figure in the inertia factor and come up with a rational
explanation of why boys have to pedal downhill when the
wind is strong. And then the spirit will leave his eyes and
he will have a story which any modern person might be
able to believe.

EXPLANATIONS

Children and adults who don't know (better) ask
   "Why."
Why does anyone die?
Why can't I always do what I want?
Why are there cows? And cowlicks?
Why is there anything at all?
Why do I hurt?
And someone who knows (better?) answers "Be-
   cause."
Because of God.
Because of the Dialectical Properties of Matter.
Because $E = MC$ Square.
Because of the Oedipus Complex.
Because of the Establishment.
Because of Male Chauvinism.
Because of anything that can be put in Capital Letters
   (like Capital or Labor).
Because of (a) and/or (b) or none of the above.
All the becauses seem pale and thin as explanations go.
Because they aren't really reasons for anything at all.
Only ways to stop the mind from gnawing on itself
   asking "Why."

Instead of enjoying cowlicks.
Or anything at all.
Or nothing.

The moral of this story is:
Just tell the story and forget the moral.
Or, don't get caught in your own explanations.

The world is a divine cypher.
We have not broken the code.

THE WILDERNESS WITHIN

A woman in a group I was leading was calm and respectable for most of the weekend. Then Saturday night "by accident" she dropped her purse into the fishpond and her supply of tranquilizers dissolved. After supper she insisted on working in the group. She began with hints that she had "regressed" in another group a year earlier. Her face contorted as she talked about her fear—a nameless terror which possessed her and drove her mad. She asked, almost demanded, some assurance of me that she could venture into her interior wilderness and return alive. I hesitated and trembled invisibly. I did not want the responsibility for being a magician who would cast out her demons. I debated with myself: "How can I play God and guarantee safe passage to this woman? She is teetering on the psychotic edge; but if I don't I confirm her fear that she is crazy, that she is a victim of forces over which she has no control." Courage or audacity or plain foolishness won the debate. "It is your wilderness," I said. "You can get lost in it and stay crazy or walk in and out of it enough times to get familiar with the territory." Her eyes seemed to focus inward on some caldron where hatred, pain and terror were seething together. She wailed like an animal. Finally her face grew hard and rage began to pour out of her: "I want to kill you. I want to kill you," she screamed. I quickly calculated the realistic danger to myself and decided to play the melodrama through to the end: "Kill me if you must." I wondered whose face she was seeing when she looked at me. She put her hands around my throat and started to squeeze. Just as I began to feel more pain than I had bargained for she crumbled into a ball and started crying: "I don't want to kill you, I don't want to kill you." As she sobbed the fear left her eyes and she began to soften. For another hour we worked. First she would go into the terror and then come out again. Then in. Then out again. In the end, she knew she held the guide rope, the thread of Ariadne, which she could follow into and out of her madness.

This incident puts me in touch with the strange country from which the Omenhawk was an emissary. Dare to explore the wilderness within and the world without also becomes surprising. The sham of rationality, the illusion of control, the cultural compromise of false sanity must be shattered before we can see the true wonder of things. The hawk came from a land ruled by synchronicities in which the deepest desires of the human personality are satisfied. We enter that land via dreams, poetic seizures, psychosis, drugs, meditation, lovemaking, ecstatic leisure, etc. It is a crazy land of unbelievable stories. I fear the violence it does to my ordinary categories of understanding and usual ways of coping. But I suspect this unknown territory is the home of the gentlest virtues. There abide (without sugar coating or dogmatic glaze) faith, hope and love. If I could visit there more often I would not have to search for recognition. I would cease performing a part on an ill-defined stage for invisible but hostile eyes. Our true identity awaits us on the other side of fear.

The fear of going too far
keeps us from going far enough.

Dream. Last night I dreamt that I came upon a turbulent body of water in which someone had drowned while skin-diving. I put on an aqualung and dove down looking for the body. I explored the sides but could find no body, so I dropped all the way to the bottom and searched in the mud. I was immediately swept away by an underground river which pushed me into a narrow shaft. I knew there was no way out and I was afraid I would drown in the same way as the person for whose body I was looking. Then I got the idea I might be able to crawl back up the shaft against the flow of the current. I blacked out. The next scene, in the dream, I was lying in a hospital bed explaining to the naval officer who had originally been directing the search for the body how I was miraculously saved from drowning.

This afternoon Howard Thurman called to tell me that our old friend Wally Pahnke drowned yesterday while skin-diving off the coast of Maine. (His body was never found.)

THE SNAKE AND I

Last night I dreamt there was a snake in the house. I picked up a stick and hit him but he only crawled under the couch. I was nervous in the dream. I knew I should not hit snakes, but I felt compelled to do so. At breakfast I talked about the dream to my friend and she suggested I should feed the snake and make friends with him if he should appear again in a dream.

After breakfast I rode into La Jolla on my motor scooter. As I was riding along the unused road next to the Torrey Pines Golf Course I met him again. In the middle of the road was the largest snake I have seen in the wild. He looked like a copperhead I once killed in Pennsylvania: about five feet long, pointed head, fat and sleek, with yellow diamond markings on his back. This time (unlike my meeting with the Omenhawk) I knew immediately that he had been sent. He was waiting for me. Otherwise why would he have been lying in the middle of the road? Or why would he have remained still when I rode my belching Vespa within reach of his nostrils? No, he was no accident. He had come to deliver the message.

My first impulse was the normal American response to noncapitalistic animals: Kill. After all, he was probably poisonous and he was on the edge of a golf course where innocent matrons played in the sun. And snakes are sinister. Enemies. Poison-bearing creatures. But remembering the dream I did nothing but shut off the motor scooter and look at him. He was clearly alive and well and waiting for me to make the next move. After a while I decided to go with magic and dreams rather than common sense and I determined I would touch him in a friendly manner to show my trust. I timidly stroked his tail. And he responded in a very snakelike manner by coiling. But he made no effort to strike. He looked at me. I looked at him. Then I began to get the message. His silence told me he had been waiting for me. His presence told me there were commandments I must obey to remain alive to the strange and holy spirit that rules this world:

Be care-ful of wild and dangerous things;
Don't domesticate the wild creatures who live in the jungle of dreams:
Don't presume to become over-familiar and control the numinous power of holy snakes or omenhawks.

Minutes later the snake uncoiled, like a fading erection, and moved with slow dignity into the bushes. We understood that we understood each other.

My brother, the snake, visited me several times in dreams in the next week and we kept a respectful distance and honored each other's powers. Two weeks after the morning of the first visitation I was walking on the beach two miles south of Del Mar (three miles from the Torrey Pines Golf Course). There he was again: five feet of snake —dead. But real as the timeless sand and the tides that had brought him to this place for burial.

By what categories may I understand this thing? Luck? Chance? Synchronicity? Omen? How do you know it was the same snake? And yes, Dr. Freud, we all know what snakes mean when they appear in dreams.

I am hesitant to label (to libel) my friend a coincidence or a phallic symbol or to reduce his length by any other explanation. Why should I baptise the event with a category which will allow me to pretend I understand the workings of this strange world?

The key to understanding everything is:
There is no key to understanding everything.

5

A New Self Borning: The Thoughtful Body and The Carnal Mind

A moment comes when there is a shift
from destruction of the old
to borning of the new.
The crisis is over.

Once I decided to go all the way
the road turned downhill toward home.

The renewal of the self has always been described by
   metaphors.
The process is poetic.
It is like:
a butterfly emerging from a cocoon;
coming out of a dark cave into the sunlight;
waking up after a nightmare;
an unexpected armistice ending an undeclared war;
a television picture coming into focus;
a bone returning to its socket;
energy surging up after a long illness;

shedding an old skin;
breathing deeply of fresh air;
being born again;
having cataracts removed;
recess;
getting to the punch line of a shaggy-dog story;
a bud emerging from the humus;
a second childhood;
becoming your own father and mother;
an ember bursting into flame;
an interior marriage between the male and female;
the fading of a mirage;
dis/illusionment;
an alchemical transformation of dross into gold;
homecoming;
For me the most helpful metaphors are political:
    liberation;
    a psychological Fourth of July;
    an end to tyranny—the tyranny of the oughts, dis-
            satisfaction, perfectionism,
            moralism, intellect.
    the overthrow of psychological capitalism in
      which the head (capital) controls the body;
    the transfer of authority (power) from outside to
      inside;
    one vote each for thought, feeling, sensation, in-
      tuition, imagination, memory, ideals and the
      moral sense.

When my mind is working like a computer
it turns me into a machine:

Black/white   Choose one
Either/or   Choose one
Right/wrong   Choose one

Good/bad   Choose one
Strong/weak   Choose one
Innocent/guilty   Choose one
         Praise grey.
         Honor dappled things.

HOW MY MIND HAS CHANGED IN THE LAST TEN YEARS

I have a fantasy I will be asked to write an article in the *How My Mind Has Changed* series. Most of the famous people who wrote in the series had no change of mind. Only a change of ideas. It is not my ideas that have changed but the way I think and the place from which I think. I once thought entirely with my head. Now I think from various centers in my body (chakras in the Hindu or Buddhist myth of the body). Heart, guts and genitals have reasons the mind knows not of. I think more from within instinct, emotion and movement. If I have a pain in the heart I listen to what that is telling me about the way I perceive and live in the world. I have not abandoned the marvelous world of ideas ("The mind is an erogenous zone."—RAQUEL WELCH), but now my mind works within the environment of my incarnate, historical life. I think more as Sam Keen and less as anyone. My mind once worked all of the time. It was filled with concepts, ideas and problems to be solved. It ran ahead of the present moment to catch any worry that might be lurking in the future. Now I shut my eyes and in the silence images and stories play in my head. Thinking is more like watching a waking dream than like working out an answer to a question.

Perhaps the largest change came from the discovery of a stationary, silent observatory within the mind from which point I can watch the constant movement of my thoughts and my life. In the Hindu-Buddhist tradition this point is called "the true-witness self." I think of it as the truth-teller within myself, the holy spirit. At any time when I am confused or pushed blindly by infantile emotions I can take the psychic elevator up to this observatory and watch what is going on with kindly and objective eyes and name things dispassionately. For instance, when I am in the middle of a fight with myself or my lover I can disassociate for a moment and ask myself about the truth of the situation.

We have a choice about the nature of consciousness, about what mind means, about the way we perceive and process the data we get from the inside and outside worlds. There are forty-two ways to see a cow or to understand a riot in Baltimore. The primal freedom of the mind is the freedom to choose how much I am to be identified with my moods, feelings, possessions, relationships, thoughts, pains, ideals. Mind changes most when I learn that I am not my mind any more than I am the fleeting pain of a headache. Whatever "I" am, . . . I am more than that. The "more than" is something that escapes definition.

My mind wanders more (my best thoughts come when I am walking), and I understand thinking as a process of exploring different modes of awareness or states of consciousness. Hard thinking is only one type of thought. My mind is just as engaged when I lie softly and simmer in bed between sleep and waking, catching the tales of the remaining dreams. Or when I project myself into a cat and try to imagine what it is like to chase a mouse. Or when I allow music to inhabit and move my body and the rhythm of the dance becomes me.

We literally make up our minds. We choose the states of awareness in which we will live the majority of the time and those we will visit only rarely. The trick is to travel widely enough in the various countries of consciousness to get an idea of the places we want to dwell and the routes for returning there. There are places in the mind that can be reached only by climbing over sheer mountains and others that can be reached only by floating down a lazy river by an old mill stream. Different people prefer different places. (Example: a simple formulation is Jung's four types—thinking, feeling, sensation and intuition.) There is a biological, sociological and neurological givenness to our make-up, our programming. Our typical mode of consciousness is shaped by early training and habit. But there is a wide margin of change permitted. Beginning again, second birth, etc., involve exploring the modes of awareness and thought that are non-typical *for you*. My adventure involved plunging into the indistinct worlds of sensation and intuition. Another person will have to take a trip into the rigors of logic and systematic thought to find freedom. To be free we each have to learn how our mind is programmed and learn to change it.

The way I think determines the relationship between my mind and my body. If everything must have a meaning I cannot entertain sensations. There is no point to a caress. Lovemaking is not significant. An orgasm has no purpose. Nothing is proven by sunlight on pine needles or the feeling of flesh on flesh. Delight does not fit into the picture frame within which purposive thought (and paranoia) would enclose experience.

INCARNATION: COMING HOME TO THE BODY

"As my consciousness has come to dwell in my body I have felt a heaviness that I first mistook for depression. A fully sensuous life-style involves knowing the essentially tragic character of the human condition—i.e. disillusionment. As I identify with my body I see the insignificance of all those substitute monuments to immortality—hoarded wealth, opulent machines, political empires, youthful facades—that we death-defying American Prometheans create.

"Each is an evasion of the primal sorrow that comes when we learn that all we love and enjoy is terribly fleeting and vulnerable. All flesh does decay, and until that knowledge comes to root in our interior there can be no real dancing. It was no accident that the Greeks, who fused Eros and Thanatos, ecstasy and death, long before Freud, were ardent devotees of the flesh and fierce enemies of death. Thus the grounding of awareness in the body is both a joyful homecoming and a heavy trip downward into the humus, the ground and end of human existence, the first and last truth."*

* Sam Keen, "My New Carnality," *Psychology Today*, October, 1970.

INCARNATION: SPIRIT COMING INTO FLESH

The great irony is that Jesus discovered the path of incarnation, the way beyond neurosis to rebirth and Christianity turned him into a savior to help people perpetuate the neurotic elements within themselves. Every person is born a high god, the only begotten child, the favorite of the father or mother. The neurotic's creed: I have hidden claims to glory; I am not like you.

It is true, my love, I have been far away, out of my body, out of touch with myself and with you. I have pretended and performed, molded myself to conform to some image of perfection. I made myself and made you, and called it making love. Admire me, the divine Marlboro Man for my self-sufficiency and independence. So hard and keen in mind and clean in heart.

My kingdom is not of this world. I am superior because in the secret kingdom of my ideals I am perfect and immortal; I don't make mistakes or fail. I and the undying Father-Mother are one. The Nicene creed was the western solution to the Oedipal problem, to the threat of death: I and the Father-on-High are One. We do not die. We are not really of this world but only missionaries to the natives sent to keep the world safe for democracy.

Jesus was a fool (Philippians 2:5). He gave the show away, gave up the pretenses, refused to be the messiah. He was crucified for refusing to be Lord and Savior. Sorry, no saviors because no damnation. No eternal domination by an absent father. His kingdom was of the earth. His humility was in refusing the illusion of purity. I am soiled, do not call me good. His secret was: there is no secret. This is where we belong. Now is our homecoming. Resign dominion over

But sterile. And why have I held myself apart from the world, afraid of merging, trusting?

Now I am flowing, coming into my body, coming into your body. I have been wooed into incarnation, educated into humility by the odors of your body, the merging unguents of our love. In the flow, in the fluid, in the juice I learn that life is not a problem which might be solved. Dissolution. Disillusionment with the ideas, schemes and high purposes. Finally, at last, at the end of time I give into you and we meet on the trembling ground of desire. In this place we touch and cease making each other over into some divine image. We love without making.

It is strange being here at home. I have come from far away to this hearth. I remember Olympus and all my gilded dreams of glory. Touch me with care. With tenderness. I surrendered my kingdom, my dominion, my claim to sufficiency to live in this moment with future kingdoms. Abdicate control that grasps for glory. Give in to the holy earth. Good-bye Olympus. Hello California, or East Orange, N.J. It's good to be home. you. And I grieve for my lost divinity. There is no salvation now. Only living and dying and merging with the abiding earth. Only this time of soft breathing together in the warmth after love.

You're nobody
till some body
loves you.

Let your body mind itself.

To be embodied is to experience everything. When I am finely tuned and in touch with myself I visit the extreme emotions of ecstasy and despair but I abide in the moderate place of contentment. In neurosis (a word I hate) there is no center, only extremes; a constant oscillation between feelings of omnipotence and impotence, pseudo-joy and theatrical despair, striving after impossible ideals and dismal failure to achieve actual satisfaction. The way out is to learn to be at home in any moment, to live contentedly for the majority of the time in the middle range of feelings. The ideal is not to be burning up with passion all of the time but to live with warmth, enjoyment and awareness. Violent passions, like summer thunder storms, are occasional graces which sweep away stale tensions and clear the air for action.

A linguistic corollary—the language of embodied life. We need to devalue certain words and revalue others; a readjustment of our linguistic economy. Overpriced, inflated words: ecstasy, fulfillment, joy, love, far out, bliss, cosmic consciousness, the human potential. Underpriced words: good, nice, kind, fine, lovely, gentle, contentment. We need to revalue those words that give dignity to the middle range of human experience. There is nothing wrong with middle-class virtues or the middle range of emotions so long as we are not exiled from the extremes. The pathology of middle-class existence is the refusal to experience the ecstasy and terror of the human condition. The pathology of the extremes is the refusal to recognize the glory of a moderate and disciplined life.

BODY LANGUAGE: WORD MADE FLESH, AND VICE VERSA

There is carnal and discarnate language, a reborn and an unborn way of speaking. When we are new our language is new. When we are not it is stale, clichéd, chatter.

Words are suspect. Advertising and propaganda have prostituted the great words. Too much noise. Too many books (this one?). Too much lying with words. Something primal in us rebels and wants more silence, more space between the words. Shorter sentences. No fat. Wow! Or perhaps only—! We can tell the truth teller by his reserve; by what he doesn't tell. The mystery is wrapped in silence.

Yet. Man is a verbal animal. Flesh and vocabulary are joined. We see, feel and speak as an integrated act. Impression and expression are diastolic and systolic. An impediment in either mode interrupts the rhythm of the heart.

Thus. The important question is not: "To speak or not to speak" but "How may my words be incarnate?" Or:

"How can the flesh be translated (not transcended)?" Or: "Can words become carnal?" The problem is to get away from mass-produced, prefabricated, plastic language. Speak as a person, not a spokesperson—an instance or a representative. No actual person is a sergeant, a press secretary, an intellectual, a Christian, a Republican.

We choose how we will live within our language. It may be facade or revelation. Much talk, perhaps most, is cover-up. The self, fearing to appear nude, wraps layer after layer of language around its tender places. Facade construction. We are like the one-horse towns in western movies. Image management. The bureau of public relations is constantly working to create the right impression, i.e. to mislead the public.

I find it easy to talk about what I have been or what I hope to become. It is much more difficult to reveal the mixed reality of the moment, to speak about the confusion and the clarity, the impotence and the power, the arrogance and the humility, the pettiness and the grandeur that are my life. It is safer to cover my real feelings and become an official person dispensing opinions and saying what will be pleasing to my audience.

The alternative is to allow language to be an expression of the moment—a cry, moan, sigh, laugh, bellow, giggle, grunt, roar. Or it may become a kind of poetry in which I marry the inner feeling of the moment with a metaphor to make a bridge between myself and another. Language may be used for making prisons or inviting love.

One trick that works for me in keeping my language within hailing distance of my experience is the linguistic fast. Any time a word has become so important to me that I notice it recurring frequently I try to prohibit myself from using it. This forces me to create new metaphors and coin language to fit my experience. For shock value: list the ten most frequently used words in any organization to which you belong (including your own personality) and force yourself to stop using them. When we experiment with a variety of ways of expressing ourselves we begin to play with the world. On the first day of creation God did nothing—except play with words.

Carnal language centers around wish, want, desire, like, delight, rather than around ought, must, duty, obligation, requirement, have to. It is erotic rather than neurotic, governed by the logic of satisfaction rather than the tyranny of oughts. In beginning again the surprise is that it is easy to be myself. The right thing is the easy thing. Or as Augustine said, "Love and do what you want." The moral act is spontaneous, rooted in the body. It emerges from what we most deeply desire. Thus the most important problem is discovering what is satisfying. We may trust pleasure to lead us to the good. (Erotic realism demands that the principle of the priority of pleasure be stated in the plural. Our pleasure, not my pleasure, is the guide.)

Turn everything topsy-turvy
Let foolishness play in your mind
Clown around with your selves

My life fits me like a glove
But sometimes I have to turn it inside-out.

The parts can't make a whole until every part has been played. We must assume many pseudonyms, inhabit many aliases before we earn the right to call ourselves by a single name. My name is legion. We are all performers. Watch the different acts at any party or in the street theater. Everywhere costume, role, gesture, the systematic creation of character. When we don't acknowledge that we create our own roles, myths, dramas, we misuse the idea of fate to force others into playing a part in our script they may not want to play. When I am able to applaud my performance I also enjoy yours. Paradoxically, the anxiety of performing ends if the play has cosmic meaning, because then we do not have to win the applause of our peers. Perhaps, God is the cosmic voyeur who applauds all performances, the universal audience who allows the play to go on.

If you must be serious
try something really hard—
give up suffering
give up working on yourself
give up improving
give up searching.

Sincerity is an overrated virtue. When practiced excessively it gives birth to self-righteousness and kills the imagination. Learn to pretend. Tell lies. Play your part in the game, don't work at it.

The answer to the problem of overpopulation is not to stop having children. It is to make fewer of them physical. Procreate all the persons who live within you. Be your own community. Be fruitful and multiply. Creative schizophrenia. Give birth to the whole cast of characters within you. God has a million faces; He, She, It, They are expert in disguise. Why not you?

We get to the real drama of life after we re/play the melodrama of childhood. The psyche is a theater. We are archetypes to each other before we become real. She was Mother and Wife and Woman to me before she became herself. Superimposed over her face were the faces of all the women who had nurtured and injured me. When we can run an instant replay of any past scene we can get on with the game of the present.

Who do you re-present?

Summer

Rest and
Ripening

fter many travels Person began to long for a resting place. At the edge of the Wilderness of Novelty s/he marked out new boundaries and defined limits to keep Chaos at bay and built a home where the gods and goddesses of the Hearth could be worshiped. The Sword of Aggression hung on the wall but Person used it less and less. Without ceasing to be a Warrior or Explorer, Person became a Homesteader who cared for the earth and tended a garden.

By now Person had lived alone so long that the Specter of Loneliness had been transformed into the Pleasure of Solitude. And since s/he was comfortable as a single one, Person risked reaching out to an Other with whom to share the tasks and joys of homesteading. Intimacy came to dwell in the home and Love blossomed again.

But Person still felt isolated, like a hero without a people, a shaman without a tribe. The more s/he moved away from private suffering into inner joy the more s/he wanted to share the boon with others. In time a Community of Travelers came together. And everyone was happy to live on the edge of the Wilderness of Novelty and work and play and take care of the land.

And Person felt rich and satisfied in the Communion of the People. On warm Summer evenings, when the work was finished, they shared a meal and danced and sang and told stories of their journeys and took pleasure in each other.

6
Limits

Playing fields have boundaries.
Games have rules.
People have limits.

Reality should be kept in its place.

Play and limits. My life is changing. I used to see everything in tragic perspective. I was filled with conflict,
seriousness, striving, moral earnestness. I worked on myself and tried harder and missed no opportunity to hold
the ideals of prophetic perfection high above the actual
failures of the social order. In the service of what ought to
be I was ruthlessly critical. The new thing emerging in
me is soft and warm and drenched in pleasure. Laughter
is rising and threatens to inundate my tragic soul. It is
getting harder to suffer. (SAMUEL JOHNSON: "I tried to be a
philosopher. But cheerfulness kept breaking through.")
Fantasy runs rampant. I simmer each morning in dreams
before I begin the day and pause a dozen times before

noon to enjoy some image that has popped unbidden into my mind. The psychedelic circus of the unconscious plays continually in my mind. I dip in and out of limitless imagery and endless possibilities. Where I once demanded explanations I now watch the shifting patterns of phenomena. I ask "Why?" less often, and wonder at the how of things.

But my frivolity sometimes worries me. Flowing, like Proteus, I change forms. There is laughter in the transformations, the gurgling of a rushing stream. But can I hold still? Can I bind time by vows? Can I commit my energies to consistent action in some unknown future? Can I establish limits that will channel my energies? I taste the delight of the world and of myself but what of the pain and conflict? *War and famine!* One face of the world is tragic. If I ignore it I become a shallow optimist. If I see it exclusively I become a dour presbyterian prophet tinged with grey self-righteousness. The trick seems to be to combine the sense of life as a task with the sense of life as a game, to remain playful in a world that is always haunted by the specter of evil. Because the world is both tragic and comic I need to remain worker-warrior and joyful fool. I need to soar into the endless possibilities of play and to focus my energies in a limited work and a specific style.

Limits, limits, what are the limits? How can I know when I am betraying myself by timidly remaining within the ancient boundaries-institutions-relationships-limits and when I am courageously cultivating the specific piece of earth I have been given? When should I honor my vows and commitments, and when should I sever myself from entanglement with the past?

When my old life tasted stale and I wanted something

new I chased a butterfly into the woods. I almost caught her; I fell exhausted; I realized I was lost and too far away to return home; I began to make a new home in the wilderness. Now, looking back, I (Adam and Prometheus my brothers) know how necessary it is to track down illusions, to test limits, to fail and to begin again. In the action that ruptures the protective walls of our home we become guilty; but we lose our shame. I cry with the knowledge that I have added to the lump of pain that burdens the earth; I have injured my children. I live with loss; but I am no longer haunted by illusions nor ruled by the authority of an absent god. By infidelity I learned (what the author of *To a Dancing God* already knew with his head) that vows may be sweet bonds that tie us to the earth. Through exile I learned that I cannot live without a home. By departing from the way pointed by my parents I learned how many of their values I cherish. I am no longer innocent. In my new and awesome world I will build walls strong enough to shield me from the terror of isolation. I cannot live alone; therefore there are limits.

To live a vital life
breathe in and out
expand and contract.
After the crisis in which the old order is destroyed
there is anxiety and chaos; darkness on the face of the
    deep.
Then excitement is born and we play with a myriad of
    possibilities.
In time there will be new decisions, new directions,
and new order
from which chaos will once again be born.
Ad infinitum
so long as life is

A life without endings
would never begin again.

A life without defense mechanisms?
Picture a nude turtle.

Harden!
Shells protect
the quick
and
the dead.

Plowing in New England: the rocks must be taken from
the center of the field and put into the wall. Growing space
for green things depends upon establishing strong boundaries.

Prometheus, you fool—
approach the limits
with tenderness
not violence.

7

We Two Are New

Love has seasons.
It will Fall
and Spring
again.

Loss and failure are mini-deaths. After disappointment I want to shrink into the dark cave of my ego and lick my wounds. I do not want to risk being vulnerable again. But, with April, healing begins and outward turning. I flow into we; my self merges into a new world; love is reborn.

C/lose
and
open
a/gain.

When desire has lain dead in the frozen sepulcher of February, nourish the tendrils wherever they reappear.

Spring is no time for timidity or morality. Trust desire to create the boundaries your new life will demand. Only a fool tries to dictate the terms on which he will allow life to retain the green edge.

Keep asking: "What do I desire?"
The other important questions will follow.

The pleasure principle: the pleasure comes before the principle.
    or   eros before logos;
    or   energy is eternal delight;
    or   God is love;
    or   trust what moves you most deeply.

If it doesn't feel good it isn't graceful.

The old moralisms about unselfish actions rest upon the mistaken belief that we can separate passion and compassion. As within so without. As I love myself so will I love my neighbor.

When falling in or out of love reclaim the projections you have put on the other person. Was s/he the source of all delight and nurture? Find levity and comfort within yourself. Was s/he strong and competent? Find your power and your vocation. We try, and fail, to possess those persons in whom we see the qualities we lack. Become what you have not been and you free your love from grasping need.

Do unto yourself as you would have others do unto you.

A *vow to myself:*

I promise to love, honor and cherish all
parts of myself, in sickness and in health, for
better or for worse, for richer or for poorer,
till death do us unite.
Without this vow there can be no lasting
marriage.

Loving
this broken self
I almost mend.

There is a darkness at the bottom of love. We are driven by the desire to merge with another. Yet each step toward the merger is taken with ambivalence—yes and no— fascination and fear. Paranoia must be faced at every threshold. The caution light flashes: DANGER, DANGER. One by one barriers and defenses must be dismantled to let another person into the citadel of privacy. The fear of being abandoned or smothered must be conquered. In matters of love, ecstasy and terror go hand in hand.

Love story:
I am still
yes
and
k(no)wing
you.

Love does not dissolve loneliness. It only makes me rich in my solitude. It is tempting to surrender responsibility for the self and merge into life-in-tandem—the Hollywood solution. But no corporate merger can relieve me of the necessity of living and dying my own life. I am a single one and merger is for a moment only. If I trade my freedom for succor we cling together and nourish each other's fears of the wilderness, excitement withers and love grows wrinkled as a limb with severed nerves.

Sometimes:
    (I) can't reach (You)
Sometimes:
    We.

Love is a drama of alienation and reconciliation, being apart and coming together. Unbroken harmony, like wall-to-wall intimacy, is usually the mark of symbiosis or defeat.

Orgasm is a metaphor.
In the flood of pleasure we lose control
and trust a current deeper than our individual wills
to sweep us downstream toward fulfillment.
A divine trickster fools us into surrendering our isolation.
Death may be the final orgasm.

The mathematics of hate: $-$ and $\div$
The mathematics of love: $+$ and $\times$

Perfection in love?
Love imperfection.

8
We Are All One Body:
The Politics of Pleasure

When we are healed we are baptized into the body
 politic.
Rebirth is moving from isolation to community.
We turn away from our private suffering to confront
 public tragedy.
Or: United we stand. Divided I fall.

Definitions. Or game plans:
Paranoia: THEY vs (i).
Nationalism, or corporate paranoia: they vs (WE).
Individualism: (I) vs you, they, it.
Communion: i and you and it and they are WE vs
 nobody.

Let your inrage turn to outrage.
4,000,000 humans, give or take a nursing child in arms
 or two, will starve to death in sub-Sahara Africa
 this year.

The United States budgets over 100 billion dollars this new year for arms (rock-a-bye baby) and "defense" alone. Over half of our expenditures are for wars— past, present or future.

Rebirth:
Turn inside-out
or love your neighbor as yourself.

THE POLITICS OF PLEASURE

Feeling is one. Indivisible.

There are no absolute boundaries between the world and the self. As within, so without. We do unto others as we do unto ourselves. The Golden Rule is a fact, not a commandment. As I enjoy or judge myself, so I will enjoy or judge the other. We are permeable or defended in the same degree as we face the outer or the inner world. This is the basis of the politics of pleasure: if I have to control myself I have to control others around me. Fascism within and without.

The idea of private pleasure. The great illusion: I want to feel for myself but not for others. The bodhisattva knows he cannot enter nirvana until all sentient beings accompany him. Passion and compassion are linked.

Breathe in and breathe out, inspiration and expiration are symmetrical parts of a cycle. The rhythm is either slow and deep or fast and shallow. Deeper in and further out are paradoxical brothers.

The Pentagon exhausts the internal economy to erect defenses against The Enemy (The Stranger, The World). Our defense establishment, character-armor, military/industrial complex guards us against trust and compassion.

What softness, tenderness and pleasure do we sacrifice to keep ourselves battle-ready?

All
pleasure
to
the
people.

PLEASURE AND POLITICS

Swans Island, Maine. 10:30 A.M. The fog is beginning to lift. The lobstermen have long since finished tending the pots that punctuate the cove in front of my (?) land. I awoke early this morning, stiff from a long night of sleeping on the ground; built a fire; made breakfast; smoked a pipe; began a day of serious loafing. If it rains there will be more to do; tend the tent and keep the fire burning. If not I will clear brush and chop some dead trees.

The rhythms that rule this place are long and comforting. The pebble beach sighs as the daily tides fill and empty the cove. The cycle of the year is marked by falling leaves and greening larches. The millenia round the jagged edges of the shore line and in time (beyond imagination) will grind the pebbles to smooth sand.

It is easy here to feel that my life is encompassed in deathless rhythms. Easy to care for myself and my people. It is hard to care about the crises which sweep the contemporary world. Washington, Vietnam, Africa are so remote.

A major problem of the moral life: how to combine private satisfaction and public dis-ease, the contentment with which the body must be nourished with the prophetic outrage which is the only appropriate reaction to the public world we have created through technology? I need to honor the circadian pulse of my body as it moves in harmony with the tides and with the body of a woman and also the staccato rhythms which rule the mad cacophony of the world of politics.

The notion of ecology requires a major re/vision of the modern mind. It assumes that everything fits together into a complex and living whole. Disturb one part of the system and everything suffers. Only respect for the whole will prevent disintegration of the parts. One world or none at all.

I find in myself a profoundly anti-ecological attitude— the assumption that I must organize and control everything. If I, the central manager of the world, do not order things properly chaos will take over. This presumption denies that I am an integral part of a system that is already organized with wisdom sufficient to keep the stars in their courses. It is the arrogant assumption that we are the controllers that has created the ecological crisis—an economy of production and consumption, waste and pollution, the pax Americana in Vietnam. Ecology must be based on trust and humility: We earthbodies belong to the cosmos.

Echology
Earthsong
The world is calling.

IF WE ARE NOT THE MANAGERS OF THE UNIVERSE WHO ARE WE?

What is our vocation? What center may our lives circle if we reject the false gods of control, possession, performance and security, and if the addiction to excitement is not enough to give us a sense of meaning? What vocation can make of life more than a series of discrete happenings to be joined, at best, by a metaphor? Perhaps: for most people there will be no vocation, only habit which muffles the appeal that is sounding through the cacophony of this time. But for those who will hear there is a cry emerging from the myriad voices of our modern madness. Our ejaculations are a static testimony to our disunity. We are fragments, splinters, fractures, diverse islands of consciousness in a lonely sea, atoms, monads whirling in parallel spaces, never touching, partisans of diverse causes sharing no communion. There is a breakdown of visual and moral constancies. The synapses no longer connect the moments of consciousness. The body-politic is schizophrenic. There is law and order, but no justice. Yet the appeal—the *vocatus*—is clear: knead the parts together, forge the connections, build bridges of trust, join the images into metaphors, bind the moments together into a new vision, bond the atoms into a new community, brood over the chaos of experience until it sings a new song. It is our pain and our schizophrenia that points toward our vocation.

Politics and ecology are vocation.
The bruised and wasted flesh of the earth
Cries out for our care.
Wonder is vocation; accept the passing
strangeness of this moment.

Autumn

*Toward the End
of the Endless Way*

ith age and ripeness Person became an honored citizen of two worlds. S/he spent much time tending the homestead and sharing the life of the land with the People. But at heart Person remained a Gypsy whose spirit was most at ease wandering through all the byways of time. Person was at home in the Present, but frequently traveled back through the winding lanes of the Past, and forward along the broad superhighways of the Future.

The years traced a map on Person's face. A universal history of adventures, a chronicle of archetypal human battles, was written in the language of crow's-feet and smile lines. Yet Person remained strangely ageless. S/he combined mature competence with the soft wisdom of age and disarming frivolity of childhood. While the journey was not finished s/he was neither ashamed of the mistakes of the past nor anxious about what challenges were yet to come.

The road into the Future stretched farther than the eye could see but Person knew the Journey would be interrupted. Somewhere ahead awaited the three Dark Presences—Death, Tragedy and Evil. At times they loomed so sinister that Person cringed in fear and tried to hide in some static pocket of time. But Grief, Love and Hope came to the rescue and filled Person with Compassion for all suffering,

Courage to fight for Change and Joy in Being. So each Autumn day Person walked forward among falling leaves into the territory of the Dark Presences. And s/he seemed to be bathed in and guided by the same Invisible Light that made the New World a place of Marvel and Grace.

9

Godsong

AN INTRODUCTION

Western religion has centered on a tragic view of the world and has led to a way of life majoring in moral seriousness, work and the rational ordering of society. God as *Logos*, the Great White Father and Maker of all things, has kept us reasonable and productive. Buddhism and Hinduism have seen the world as divine and have encouraged the view of life as a game. Western religion has traditionally become bogged down in joyless righteousness while Eastern religion has ignored the problem of evil (I oversimplify).

To think is to use analogies and metaphors which both reveal and obscure reality. All analogies tumble when pushed:

> When the metaphors of seriousness, work, morality, responsibility are used to interpret life as a whole it becomes difficult to play, dream, loaf, love, wonder and accept grace;

> When the world is seen as divine play and life as a game it becomes difficult to confront tragic limitations

and wage war against the blatant evils of hunger, injustice and carnage.

The problem of work and play, of tragedy and comedy, has been central to the changing images of myself. I took the occasion of an invitation to write an essay on the play theology of Jürgen Moltmann to deal with the problem of tragedy and evil. In *godsong* I wrestle with the unsolvable mystery of evil from two radically different perspectives which are suggested by one playful and one morally serious experience. The experiences: a psychedelic vision in which images played within my mind and I was taken up into the embrace of Kali, the goddess of creation and destruction, and I knew that death and tragedy were finally encompassed by love; and the nauseating experience of having to kill a badly injured kitten on the highway.

This essay is included in *Theology of Play* (Jürgen Moltmann, Harper & Row, 1972). Moltmann angered me because there was no fun, laughter or sensuality in his thesis. And the medium *is* the message.

godsong should be chanted rather than read silently.

GODSONG

a little pro-fun-ditty about g(o)od and (d)evil

Come play with me.
What would we play?
A game.
Are there rules?
No. It's just for fun.
What is the name of the game?
Every-body plays.
Then do I have to play?
You are free.

The pointless point of fooling
round and round with
g(o)od and (d)evil is
to turn the world
topsy-turvy.
Bottoms up.
Apple basket turnover.
Vision and revision is
only revolution,
a play on wor(l)ds
with no necessary oughtcomes.
So don't take it seriously.
Whether the world is:

>   topsy
>   or
>   turvy
>   hardly matters to a bird

                                        or a bee
                                        or a bush
                                        or a tree
But it does to me.
I keep turning it over
hoping (against despair so deep it seems certainty)
by turning, turning it will come round right
it will prove itself the best of all possible worlds.
But the best the topsy or turvy world manages is
to be the best of all actual worlds
where evil still lurks in the hearts of men
(Oh, the Shadow knows).
And the actual is less than I
hoped for
counted on
demanded.
So I will do a little number
play with things
till they come round right
closer to the heart's desire.

Let's give it a whirl
a twist, a spin.
Round and round she goes.
Where she stops nobody knows
Topsy-turvy. Here we go.

Once upon a couch
spaced out in endless time
(whether with or without chemical aid is beside the point
since transubstantiation might take place in the acid
as easily as in the host)
I saw the (d)evil face
of all that is and was and might yet be.

I knew clearly and distinctly
that all things are bound together
deathly tight
by the web of necessity.
And in the prison of cause and effect
will is but an illusion
love a conditioned response
hope a placebo.
For the topsy world is ruled
by struggle, suffering, and tragedy.
And death is no escape from bondage
for we come again, and again
into the flesh.
Reincarnation, reincarceration:
another life, another death,
another spin of the wheel.
And I, caught in the endless cycle,
undigested in the cancerous gut of the inevitable world,
am condemned
to repeat, to repeat, to repeat, to repeat, to repeat, to repeat
to stutter through an eternity
of futile forms.
I think it is called paranoia
or damnation
or the logical end of seriousness
or mistrust.
In the topsy world
you have to play
a loveless game.
All rules
and no fun.

Then
fast as a speeding bullet
in a flash

in the twinkling of an eye
(with, yes, a trumpet or two)
the world turned
turvy.
I saw the joke,
the trick.
(She turned the trick on me)
And (gracious me)
I laughed
just in the old nick of time
just in the crack of space.
And I was
for the time of being
saved.   Go with it.
                Go with it.
                Go with it.
                You can have everything
                if you let yourself be.
                Out of the whirl
                Down the rapids

Now for a brief word from my sponsor
A word
(I am just playing on The Word)
about the nameless one
who wakes and sleeps
in the g(o)odness of the turvy world
that turns us on and over and
round and round.

In the first place She is black.
Or at least a little swarthy
and a lot comely.
And She doesn't carry stoned commandments.

114

But wait. I am getting ahead of my story.

When	turning in the belly of the whale
	circling in the eddy of the cosmos
	shivering in the frigid universe
	writhing in suspicion and fear
	(They are all out to get me
	They are all out to get me
	They are all out to get me)
I consented	to try no more
	to surrender
	to lie silent
	to melt
	to die (a little)
I rose up	riding the cycles of the recurring worlds
	like an acrobat balancing on the tenuous edge of time
I ascended	mounting the pulsations of increasing excitement
I embraced	the (d)evil body of necessity
	and allowed fate to have her way with me.
And she	Shiva-like held me in her arms and
tricked me	with sweet unguents of love
into coming	forth from the womb of possibility into the matrix of time
again into life	with waves of delight in which ego died and
after death	freedom was rising from the sepulcher of fate.

And I knew   the world was a single divine orgasm
                and

she did it   (but who is the actor and who's the
                act?)

because   (there is no cause when we are one)

she loved me   And her face, once strange, became
                familiar
                And the g(o)odness of the turvy
                world was redolent of the musk (the
                must) of lovers coming together on a
                rainy autumn morning.

And there you have it,
The secret is out
The trick is turned
This turvy world is
a g(o)odly playground
(and evil a parenthesis).

You who were my enemy
come out and play with me   shout down my rainbarrel
                        slide down my cellar door

Come out, come out, wherever you are.
All-e All-e in free.
No more hide-and-seek.
Everybody home free.
Come home now.
Come together.
Be (abide) with me
the darkness in the I deepens.
I. I, I, alone, must die.
We, we, we, all the way
home is where the flesh is.
When a body meets a body

116

coming through
       the dying and the living
       flowing together
       the ice melting
       the world thawing out
       And old time is tickling us with possibility
       And hope is rising young as laughter.
And now I know why
St. John (that dirty old man)
said God was a four-letter word
and Hegel (the shameless logician)
thought the world was God's plaything.
Can't you see what careless love can do?

        "Stop it. Stop it. . . ."
(An out-of-sight voice interrupts my play.
The accent is Germanic,
the vocabulary academic,
the mood anger)
"Stop this nonsense. You have an obligation to be serious and responsible. What you have given us so far is a lot of semi-erotic talk masquerading as theology. It is frivolous, flip and irreverent. Theology proper has to do with God's revelation of himself in Jesus Christ. And play becomes possible only when we understand that the creative God plays with

Jesus loves me this I know for the Bible tells me so Little ones to

The things that you're liable to read in the Bible they ain't necessarily so.

his own possibilities and
creates the world out of
nothing. And we may play
only when we know God's
purpose. Jesus suffered
that we may laugh again.
(come to Church and Play.
J.C.'s Place.
The only TRUE game in town.)

him
belong
they
are
weak
but
he
is
strong.

O.K.
I will be serious.
I solemnly swear:
To tell the truth, the whole truth and nothing but the
    (literal, constipated) truth.
To smile only on off-duty hours.
To do my duty to God and my country.
To think in straight lines.
To keep my hands above the table at all times.
To joke only about matters that are of minor import.
To take cold showers whenever I have warm thoughts.
To disregard the seduction of unconscious associations.
To keep the faith of my fathers
To avoid low puns.
And
If I should die before I wake
I pray the Lord my soul to take
(if he can still find it
once the laughter is gone).
I Sam Keen (being of sound mind and body?)
herewith state these intentions:
The following reflections upon what is traditionally called
the problem of theodicy (See Augustine, Hume, Camus, et
al) or the ontological status of evil are designed to raise the
question of the appropriateness of the category of comedy

as a paradigmatic interpretation of the human condition
as a whole.
Or, as they might say down at the docks,
What are you laughing for, man, when you know the
bastards are going to get you in the end?
Let's play it another way
and give the devil his due.
Give it a twist
a flip of the wrist
and over she goes again.
Revolution as revelation.
Turn things topsy
and death shall have dominion
and the lower things
ass-end up on high.
A little play in three acts

Setting.
Once upon a highway
smack in the middle of the U.S. of A.
The morning is crisp as a waffle and
coming on sweet as maple syrup.

Cast (of actors?)
2 cars. 2 drivers. (One a philosopher who, for private
and professional reasons, is wondering whether it
might be possible to play in this seriously troubled
world) 1 kitten. (small size) The devil (perhaps)

Act I.
A kitten (where did it come from?) all tiger-striped is
strutting on the concrete stage of actual life, innocent
as in-fancy and maybe chasing a butterfly across the
zoomway.

Act II.
A car, presumably controlled by a reasonable and even

kindly man going to a necessary place in an efficient manner, encounters the above-mentioned kitten. Or in the vernacular, squashes it all over the goddamn highway.

Act III.
The kitten lies in a growing pool of blood and kicks away its ebbing life. The driver of the second car sees that there is nothing humorous to be done when pain and death wrestle for possession of the body. So, tenderly, he repeats the violence of the first driver and gives death a speedy victory.

Afterward the mourning is soggy with nausea and inevitable guilt. A few miles later only a little blood remains on the genuine four-ply-safe-at-any-speed-plexiglass-belted-tires.

And now mr. god
I have a question.
What is the joke?
I got the punch line
but it doesn't seem funny.
It was only a mini My Lai
a tragedy on a very small stage
but suddenly everything is
topsy with evil.
The world is a killing ground
(life is a parenthesis in a
deadly sentence)
and mr. devil is the boss.
Oh, it is a serious business.
And what is there left to say?
When the night vision blinds us
no arguments, explanations,
philosophies, theodicies

120

can erase the blood from
the concrete stage of history.
Nothing abstract or theoretical
can turn the world turvy.

Silence.
Waiting.
Surely as spring
the world will turn again.
Though why or how
I do not know.
Or even when.
In the ripeness of time
(after death)
the play will begin again
                    and
          Beginning again: the res-erection of the flesh.

When, perhaps
(for it is never certain)
and for instance
my lover's hand
or a summer wind might
touch my wrist
and travel up my warming arm
till fingers play in my hair
like seals in a whitecapped sea
and delight may certainly
(for it is always probable)
tease me away from death
and I would be satisfied
with the bittersweet days of my unfolding
and I might wonder
if death like love

is a godsong
playing through us all.
Maybe.

    Come play with me.
    What would we play?
    A game.
    Are there rules?
    No. It's just for fun.
    What is the name of the game?
    Every-body plays.
    Then do I have to play?
        You are free.

10
Time and Time Again

As the crisis ends I emerge into a new world
of possibility and action.
Time is a gift, no longer something to resent, or grasp,
or dread. I re-member the past with gratitude because it brought me to this moment.
I look to the future with excitement because
it allows me an open space in which I am free to
become.
I take pleasure in the present moment because it is the
meeting point of all that has been and might yet be.
Healing restores memory, hope, and the capacity for
joy.

(In cancer the DNA "forgets" the code which allows the
individual cells to perform in harmony with the total body
program. To heal the body is to restore its memory for
the natural order of things.)

Your past
just disappeared.
Now what?

The future begins when I cease to rehearse old scenes in which I recited lines written for me by the directors. When I become my own playwright I act in a drama I helped to create. The play begins when I become the author, the authority, of my own life.

hearse: a harrow; vehicle for conveying the dead to the grave.

To re-hearse is
to carry dead bodies
in the mind
again and again.
A grave,
harrowing experience.

If it's alive
don't hearse it.
If it's dead
don't re-hearse it.

We are shaped more
by what is not yet
than by yesterday.

The vacuum more than the thorn
in the flesh makes us who we are.
The not-yet may be a place of hope or despair.
Stay hungry for the future, but be nourished
by past and present. We are moved by
the promise of a fulfillment that is forever
slightly beyond our grasp. The trick is to
enjoy reaching without grasping.

THE CHASE

There is excitement in pursuit. We are always running after the not-yet. Hope is the opposite of pragmatism: a bird in the bush is worth two in the hand. It is what we can glimpse but cannot catch that draws us onward into the future. The quarry moves us. We are motivated by something that is missing.

But what is a hunt without a capture? It's no fun being chaste and never caught. Discontent grows when we ignore what is rich and full in the moment and concentrate too much on what is missing. There is a delicate balance between hope and gnawing discontent, excitement and nervous exhaustion. Perhaps the balance can only be maintained if we hunt for the right quarry. What quarry can sustain excitement for a lifetime? My soul (possible self) always runs slightly ahead of me. I am always becoming myself. Or, perhaps, the hidden goal of human history is the true quarry. Here is a clue. The problem with marriage or settled relationships is that the excitement of the hunt is lost (or changed into war games) unless the partners are involved in a quest that transcends the relationship. Male and female wolves hunt together in a far-ranging way.

Identity crisis:
Time hold still!
I'm not ready yet
to leave childhood
to grow older
to be strong and tall.

Resist the flow
Time grows
stagnant.

Growing
is
growing older.

Grow B/old gracefully

WRINKLES, LINES AND CROW'S FEET—REFLECTIONS ON THE AMERICAN IDEOLOGY OF AGING

Mirror, mirror on the wall,
Who is the fairest of them all?
The mirror as the place of judgment.

Each time I pass before the jurisdiction of my reflected image I am tempted to despise the actual. The mirror tempts me to equate my being with my appearance. I am over forty. Lines etch my face: perpendicular paranoic creases above the bridge of the nose; parallel furrows across the forehead like roads leading into zones of combat. The lineaments of my history, traced in my flesh, are now ineradicable. The evidence of how I have lived cannot be disguised. The creases and crow's-feet testify to eyes strained, keen, focused, trying too hard to see the future, to penetrate the unknown. As if anything beyond the reach of vision could not be trusted.

Vanity desires a virginal face upon which time has not scrawled, a face bare of lines as the map of an unexplored territory. My gnostic self, afraid of time and matter and death, would like to erase the battle scars that mark my body.

In America:

Youth is beauty (that's all we know of immortality).

We idealize the uncharted face, worship the body that is not gnarled by labor or marked by childbearing or disease.

Age mellows whiskey and cures ham, but takes the power from a man and the beauty from a woman.

Youth is truth.

Pursue it.

Dread its passing, O ludicrous California grand-mothers in mini-skirts and old men in bellbottoms, ancient bodies stumbling while trying to strut. (What happens to old peacocks?)

It's not biology but ideology that makes a sadness of old age in America. Exercise and good diet allow vitality to be maintained into advanced age. We have dispelled the myth that old age is sexless. Shame in aging comes from the fear of incarnating, the dread of limitation, the prejudice against gnarledness. The gnostic dream of the ethereal person is to keep all possibilities open, to be able to move at any moment in any direction. Life must be utopian and flawless or we will turn our eyes aside. We exile the old to leper colonies (Sun City) because they are an embarrassing reminder that actual life is never ideal and we never catch the perfection we run after. No person actualizes the full human potential. No society is utopia. With all its power, technology and money America has come no closer than the ancients to creating the alabaster city undimmed by human tears. But we insist upon happy endings and we avoid the wisdom that is embedded in tragedy. The old ones destroy the illusion upon which the American game is based—progress forever; we are in control. They show us that triumph is inevitably followed by failure as death is the certain conclusion of life. To be is to fail. And we miss the beauty of the half of life that is in the waning. If we were to question our ideology of age we might discover that the time of ripening was the richest and most powerful of all. Ancient and Eastern wise men believed life began at forty. They thought of youth as a disease from which the wise man had been cured. . . .

A FANTASY OF AGE

How would I like to think and feel about my life twenty years from now in my middle sixties?

Sam Keen, 1995. I have grown more fully into my name, earned my character. Now I see the world not as anyone might but as the somebody I have become. All my years have woven together rich patterns of experience. I see and feel things as a seasoned man. I have simmered my experience. I can open myself to a range of novel experiences that would have terrified me when I was forty. I have survived much and I now know that pleasure does not need to be rationed so strictly nor pain avoided so carefully as I once thought. My energies are smaller but more concentrated, and I don't dissipate them on insignificant things. It is easier to say no and yes without qualification or apology.

Looking back I remember my fortieth year. At forty I was in the adolescence of my maturity. I was not quite so serious as I had been at thirty, but I was taking my new-found frivolity rather grimly. Nevertheless it was a year of liberation, a time of passage into a new life. I believe that most people are not able to begin living their unique lives until they near mid-life. Until forty I was (unknown to myself) living out the unfulfilled lives of my parents. There were ghosts, autonomous complexes, demons, neurotic compulsions (pick your favorite categories) in charge of my life. Not until my mid-thirties did I begin to understand: the virtues I inherited from my parents blinded me; my color was a reflection of the radiance of my father; my morals were his fears transmuted into rules; my religious passion was a covert effort to win the approval of my mother; my quest for fame was a response to my grandmother's worship of my precociousness. At forty I began to exorcise these ghosts. No doubt my son Gifford and my daughter Lael will do battle in the dark with faceless forces for half of their lifetime before they kick me out of their pysches. I hope I may live to see them celebrate independence day.

🌿

Hope:
An Easter sandwich—life(death)life

🌿

If you were mortal
what would you do today?

🌿

Today:
a present
for you

🌿

Hear
This
Now

🌿

Beginnings

The end (*telos*) of life is now.
Today it all begins . . . again.

It is tempting to end neatly, to tie the loose ends, to sum
up the tale and add an appropriate moral. But nothing
living is tidy.

The homesteader wants thick walls, settled covenants
and well-simmered wisdom. I need a home, a world small
and hidden enough to embrace with care. In September I
bought an old house in Muir Beach within sight of the
ocean. It has more rooms than I can occupy alone. My
children visit and fill it with teenage excitement and chaos.
I share the house with a woman who is full and juicy as a
winesap apple. We have planted a garden. This morning
while we were having tea a red-tailed hawk swooped down
and picked up a garden snake from the side yard and
perched in the pine tree watching us as he ate his squirming breakfast. For the moment things are quiet.

But the gypsy is always restless. Come Winter and he
will take to the road again to explore unknown places. I

need adventure, a world too large to domesticate or comprehend. Periodically I need to be lost in a wilderness without boundaries where I feel the quickening of fear and excitement. I do not know who I may become.

So long as there is hope there will be no absolute endings. If, by grace and grit, I live as I want I will end in the middle, still ready to —————————